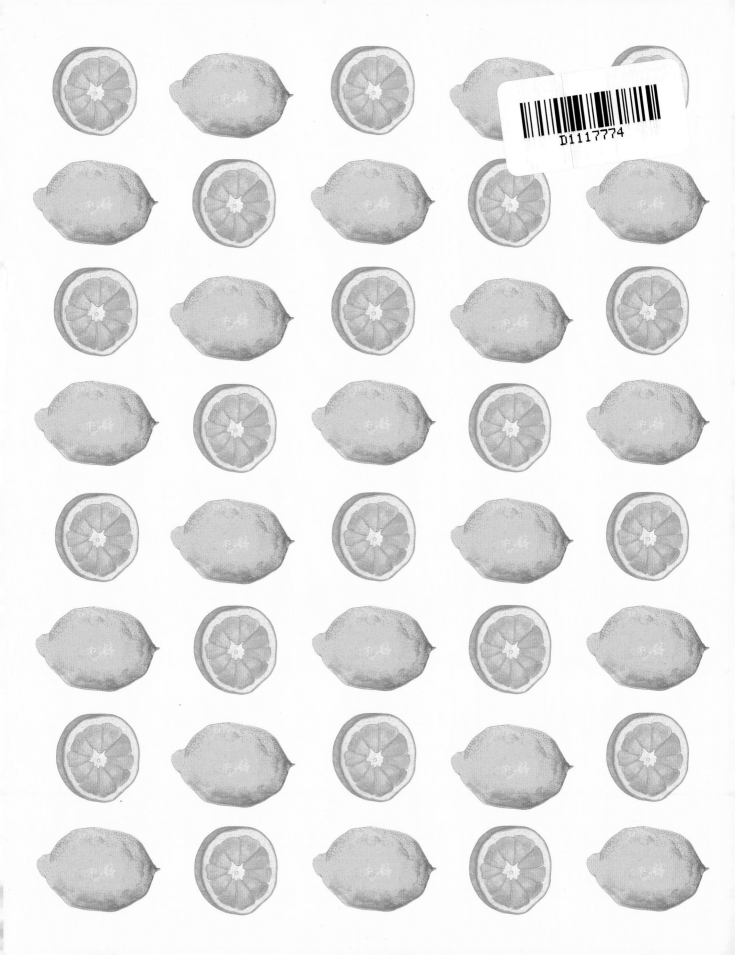

# a CURIOUS Harvest

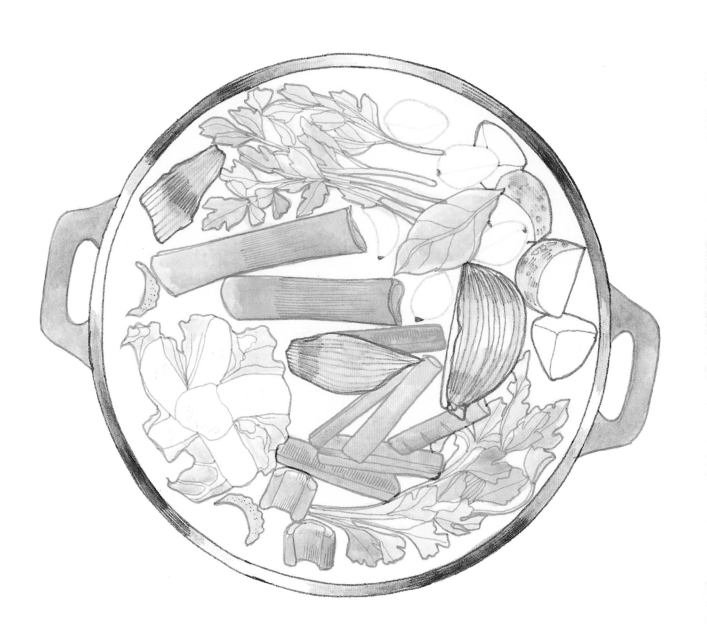

# a CURIOUS Harvest

## *the* Practical Art *of* Cooking Everything

**MAXIMUS THALER**

**ILLUSTRATED BY DAYNA SAFFERSTEIN**

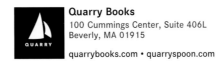

**Quarry Books**
100 Cummings Center, Suite 406L
Beverly, MA 01915

quarrybooks.com • quarryspoon.com

© 2014 by Quarry Books
Illustrations © 2014 Quarry Books
Photography © 2014 Kate Lewis Photography

First published in the United States of America in 2014 by
Quarry Books, a member of
Quarto Publishing Group USA Inc.
100 Cummings Center
Suite 406-L
Beverly, Massachusetts 01915-6101
Telephone: (978) 282-9590
Fax: (978) 283-2742
www.quarrybooks.com
Visit www.QuarrySPOON.com and help us celebrate food
and culture one spoonful at a time!

10 9 8 7 6 5 4 3 2 1

ISBN: 978-1-59253-928-4

Digital edition published in 2014
eISBN: 978-1-62788-042-8

Library of Congress Cataloging-in-Publication Data

Thaler, Maximus.
  A curious harvest : the practical art of cooking everything /
by Maximus Thaler ; Illustrated by Dayna Safferstein.
     pages cm
  Includes index.
  ISBN 978-1-59253-928-4
  1.  Food--Popular works. 2.  Cooking--Popular works.  I. Title.
  TX355.T43 2014
  641.5--dc23
                              2014004537

Cover and Book Design: Debbie Berne
Illustrations: Dayna Safferstein

Printed in China

*This book is dedicated to the Tufts University Crafts House*
*and all Crafties past, present, and future.*

# contents

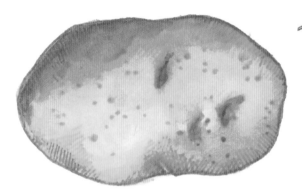
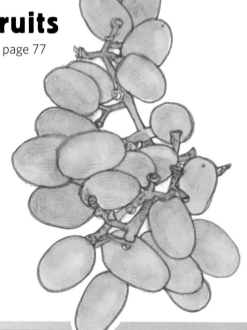
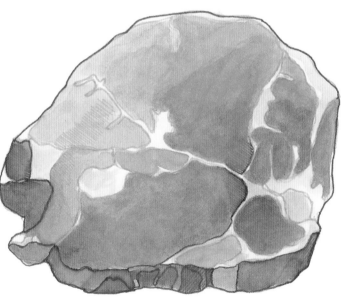

## dairy
page 97

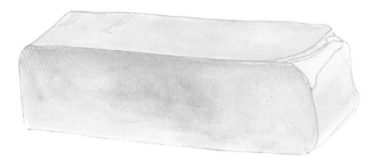

## fats
page 103

## flavorers
page 109

### flavoring vegetables
page 110

### sweeteners
page 119

### spices
page 122

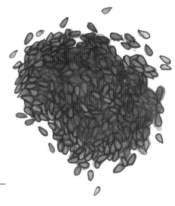

### herbs
page 137

# introduction

●┈┈┈┈┈┈┈┈┈●

**THE BOOK YOU HOLD IN YOUR HANDS** is not about finished dishes, but about raw ingredients. Think of it as choose-your-own-adventure cooking. Each of the proceeding pages contains a beautifully illustrated ingredient. I hope that you will page through them for their artistic value alone (there's much more to food aesthetics than pretty packaging). For each ingredient, there are short tips on how to prepare it, as well as suggestions of what other ingredients it might go well with. Carrots might lead you to quinoa, quinoa to garlic, garlic to kohlrabi. Flip through the pages, and synergies will reveal themselves and vegetable medleys will unfold, all without a single recipe compelling you to go out and buy that missing ingredient. There are no measurements to follow, no timers to keep track of. This book gives cooking inspiration, not cooking dogma. The point is to cultivate an intuition on how to prepare and combine ingredients, so that the back of the fridge starts to reveal possibilities rather than limitations.

My aim is to provide a methodology for regaining a relationship with your food. Food is a deeply personal thing. We bring food inside us, and then it becomes us, and we become it. Yet despite the necessarily intimate union we enter into with our food every day, few of us know where our food comes from, what it is made of, or how it will affect our bodies.

Over the past hundred years, with the help of refrigeration and other preservative processes, supermarkets became a standard feature of our landscape. A supermarket is a truly incredible thing. Food from all over the world is now wrapped in plastic and beautifully arrayed on refrigerated shelves. Anything you want is just a fifteen-minute drive away. This wealth of choices has fundamentally changed our relationship with our food. Increasingly, when people walk into their kitchens, the question on their mind is "What do I want to eat?" instead of the older question "What do I have to eat?"

At first glance, it is difficult to see the consequences of this shift. Much could be written about how supermarkets and industrial agriculture have improved our standard of living. But nothing is gained without something lost, and I am constantly surprised by how many people are unaware of what we have traded away in exchange for strawberries in February.

In short, we have lost a relationship with our food. When we ask ourselves "What do I want?" we tend to think of products, finished dishes—vegetable lasagna, Wheat Thins, or General Tso's chicken—that might satisfy our particular craving. We rummage around for our preconceived meal, and if we can't find what we want, we go out and buy it. Even those of us that are dedicated cooks are subject to this style of thinking. A lifetime wandering through aisles of brightly colored advertisements has allowed us to forget that eggs don't actually come from cartons—they come from chickens.

It boils down to a question about choice. To some, the choice between Wheat Thins and saltines may seem significant. Their branding proclaims that each has a different crunch, weight, and texture. Yet each product is simply a mixture of wheat, oil, and salt. When we pay attention to ingredients, the choice between brands becomes less of a choice. The plethora of options the supermarket aisles present makes it easy to ignore the choices we are no longer allowed to make.

When we ask "What do I want?" we isolate our decisions to the final stage in food production. We may choose between Ritz and Triscuits, but in doing so we implicitly choose to buy our food in the form of a packaged product. By asking "What do I have?" we start to reclaim our personal role in food production, and a whole host of potential choices opens up. Where do our ingredients come from? How are we going to combine them? What methods will we use to cook them? Whom will we eat them with? These are all ancient questions that until very recently every human asked before eating. I believe we need to continue asking them. They foster a full relationship between us and what we put into our bodies. This book provides answers to those questions for just about any raw ingredient you might encounter, be it in the grocery store, on the farm, in a CSA box, or even in the Dumpster.

## DUMPSTER DIVING

The first time I went Dumpstering was at a juice distribution center. The distributor had to throw away juice that had been received too close to its expiration date to be sold or that had otherwise been damaged in shipment. Hundreds of gallons of juice ended up in the Dumpster every night, and we went to go get it.

The Dumpster was quite taller than we were—we had to climb up the outside and literally dive in.

Heaped inside were juice containers and cardboard boxes, about three feet thick. Some were empty, open, or cracked, but most were completely sealed. It smelled like rot and alcohol, and I could see a shallow pool of fermenting juice below my feet. But the pool was less than an inch deep, so even when we got to the bottom, my clothes never got wet.

We had to work quickly, grabbing an empty cardboard box and filling it with as many containers as it could hold. I greedily sifted through hundreds of bottles of strawberry, mango, orange, and carrot juice. On the lid of each plastic jug was a price tag. The pints were labeled $2.99 and the quarts $7.99. My mind boggled as I did some crude multiplication and realized that we were packing up literally thousands of dollars' worth of juice.

In the end, there was too much to fit into the car, so we had to leave some behind. On the ride home, I was exhilarated. The entire process—the clandestine midnight gathering, the foreignness of the distribution center, and the otherworldliness of the Dumpster within it, the mountain of juice and meaningless price tags, the risk of being caught—all of it presented a captivating new way of looking at food and at

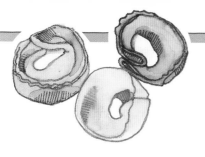

waste. I remember driving home, sipping on a mango smoothie, and pondering the $2.99 price tag. I thought to myself, "I am never buying juice again." It took a few more dives before that thought turned into "I am never buying food again."

## COMMUNAL LIVING AT CRAFTS HOUSE

So what exactly did we do with enough juice to fill a few bathtubs? We brought the juice to our collective house called The Crafts House. Crafts' structure was suited quite well to handling these sorts of harvests—the culture revolved around sharing food. We pooled our money to buy communal food, so the kitchen was completely shared. Someone was always cooking. I would frequently wander into the kitchen at 3 a.m. to find a few overcaffeinated Crafties procrastinating from their essays by baking cookies. Eating together was central to our identity. Every night at 6 p.m., two Crafties would cook and serve an open dinner.

Just before 6 p.m., the doorbell would begin to ring and guests would file in. Soon the cooks would come out and yell "DIINNEEERR!!!" at the top of their lungs. As the common room filled up, a sort of transformation would occur. College students are busy and often very self-involved. But for a brief period of every day each of our personal identities was partially subsumed by the identity of the house. At dinner, house residents and guests alike were all Crafties, sharing a meal together.

It was impossible to say whom the food belonged to in these gatherings: who was giving and who was receiving. Certainly, one could follow the technicalities—the food was purchased by Hallie or Dumpstered by Rachael, cooked by Nick, and eaten by Dayna—but that kind of reduction seemed to miss the point somehow. The meal was facilitated by the existence of the house as an entity just as much as by any of the cooks or diners. Crafts provided a space and social structure for this kind of sharing of food to occur. In some sense, it was more accurate to say that the meal was given to us by the house itself. The house fed us, and we were its body, or perhaps its soul. This soul was an amalgamation of the identities of the residents, but there was also something distinct, an independent spirit of the house.

One thing that spirit has given me is the belief that food is not a commodity to be bought and sold; nor is it simply a vessel for transporting fuel into our systems. Food is something to be shared, to build community around. Giving food to one another was how we showed that we valued each other's presence. It was a medium of shared creation.

Crafts House was a place of craft, that is to say, art, but it is a mistake to conceive of art as confined to specific media like paper or clay. Cooking was one of many ways at Crafts that we conceived of art not as a specialized activity meant for museums and galleries, but as a way of being, a way of looking at the world. Art was everywhere. From faces conjured in the wood grain of our table to the glitter permanently soaked into our floor, no surface was without ornamentation. Each drunkenly scrawled doodle or Dumpstered bread sculpture was itself a display of individual skill and creativity, but all together they amounted to something more. Like the food shared each night, it was impossible to say just who exactly owned or even produced much of the art that suffused the building. Of course you could see examples of a particular Crafty's style in specific places, but it was the totality of everyone's work together,

each bit of creation nestled in with all the others, that brought the house to life.

### VALUE

Immersed in this sense of community—of shared food, shared space, shared property, and shared creation, it felt perfectly natural to Dumpster dive. Food simply wasn't meant for Dumpsters. The food culture at Crafts allowed us to see uses for Dumpstered food that other people didn't. There's this funny phenomenon that occurs where things that are useless in small quantities become very useful when you have enough of them. For a consumer cooking for just one or two, a mushy tomato seems like garbage. It's mealy; the texture is all wrong—it's awful in a salad. But a dozen mushy tomatoes can be used to make a wonderfully "fresh" tomato sauce—fresh, that is, compared to the stuff most people buy in jars. Often, stores threw food away because their customers didn't have the luxury to operate on the same scale that we could at Crafts, and so they failed to recognize when something was still useful.

In general, usable food found its way into Dumpsters because the stores throwing it out weren't in the business of selling usable food, but of selling prepackaged products. Consumers are given a wealth of choice, so even the slightest damage to a package means that it will be passed over in favor of pristine goods. We would commonly find cartons of eggs with one egg cracked. No one will buy eleven eggs when they could get a dozen for the same price without the mess, so the damaged carton gets tossed, even though there is perfectly good food inside it.

Among the bits of packaging and food there were also price tags. We would find unused rolls of stickers, each blankly declaring what would have been the value of food that was now covered in trash. After a dive, it became a ritual of mine to fry up the most expensive meat we found. At 2 a.m. I would eat filet mignon or wild scallops and try to figure out for myself just how much that meat was worth to me. Steak was valuable certainly ($16.99, apparently?), but the grocery store had decided it was worthless because it wasn't sellable anymore. There was some disconnect between the concepts "valuable" and "sellable," or perhaps between "sellable" and "usable." I found the steak valuable because I had a use for it, while the store could not value it because it could not be sold. But the only reason I had a use for the steak, and everything else we Dumpstered, was because I had access to a very large kitchen with lots of storage and lots of mouths to eat the excess. And I had access to that kitchen, by and large, because my surely overpriced college tuition was being paid for by a scholarship from the US government, whose health codes were largely responsible for the steaks' presence in the garbage in the first place. So what on earth was the value of the steak?

The contents of the Dumpster forced traditional concepts of value into question. By sifting through the trash, it seemed like I was able to see something that no one else could see. It felt like I had empirical evidence that the value of things was not what everyone thought it was. Or perhaps I had evidence that the value of things was *exactly* what everyone thought it was, and nothing more. Dumpstering allowed me to give in to my greedy, materialistic tendencies in a way that felt entirely productive. I could covet everything, but because so much of what I owned came from the trash, I wasn't terribly attached to any of it. I was just as pleased to give things away as I was to acquire them. More pleased, actually, and the fact that I could freely give away Dumpstered items increased their value in my mind.

What I came to understand was that value is a highly subjective and multidimensional property. There are many ways to measure the value of an item, and measurement in one dimension does not exclude measurement in another. The grocery stores, by insisting that value and sellability were synonymous, were translating that multidimensional texture of an item's value into a single green metric of money, and something very important was being lost in translation.

Money is valuable because it is easily exchangeable. But, just because money is easily exchanged does not mean that it is the only medium which value can be transferred through. After some thought, I decided that I would try to create my own medium of exchange—a medium that was capable of transferring value forms that were more complex and subjective, and less quantifiable, than money. And so I began working on The Gleaners' Kitchen.

### THE GLEANERS' KITCHEN

The Gleaners' Kitchen was meant to be a community space—a place where people could come and freely exchange ideas and of course, share food. I used Crafts House as my prototype. One of the things that fascinated me about Crafts was how distinctive the physical space was. The moment you walked through the door it was apparent that you were in another world, where the rules were different. I wanted The Gleaners' Kitchen to have the same otherworldly feel, but more consciously and deliberately cultivated. Instead of a college dorm filled with kooky people, The Gleaners' Kitchen would be a bona-fide Dumpster restaurant. Like Crafts, dinner would be served every night at 6 p.m. In addition, we would be a grocery distribution center and a cultural hub. There would be concerts, poetry readings, academic lectures, and craftivist workshops. Everything would be structured to facilitate a public conversation about value that I had been having in private with the Dumpster for years.

Nothing facilitates that conversation about value better than a shared meal of Dumpstered food. It was essential to me that The Gleaners' Kitchen feel not like a restaurant, but like a home—an alternative to the world outside and a collaborative space for making change using art and food as building blocks. I wanted to invite people into my home and share with them all of the wealth that society had left behind.

I chose the name "Gleaners" very deliberately, as a connection to our agricultural roots. Where the biblical Ruth once gleaned in the fields, we now gleaned in Dumpsters, but the feeling was the same. For ancient gleaners, every waking moment revolved around acquiring food, preparing it, processing it, and sharing it with loved ones. While a biblical agrarian lifestyle is not possible today, an intimate relationship with our food still is. There is something essential about living close to food in this way that most city dwellers have forgotten.

In the time before there were any grocery stores, people were much more familiar with what was good food and what was not. The advent of chemical preservatives and pasteurization did wonders for limiting the spread of illness, but it also allowed people to stop trusting their senses. A food's "goodness," once an objective quality to be confirmed by sight, scent, and flavor, transformed into an amorphous property to be manipulated by advertisers. But in the Dumpster, all the food advertisements had decayed, leaving only the raw ingredient underneath, food essence, ready for evaluation.

Dumpster diving is a way to reconnect to our agrarian past in a modern context. Our pastoral mythologies are lush with stories of transformation, of death and resurrection. In the spring, dead earth is transformed into living sustenance. In the autumn, the plants wither and rot away, leaving nothing but a seed and the promise of rebirth next year. Dumpstering carried with it this mythological resonance. It was a way of transforming what others thought was dead and decaying into something new and life giving. We saw ourselves as society's kidneys, filtering its waste and reassimilating what we could. The human city is still an emerging organism, and we strove to close its open loops. The Gleaners' Kitchen aimed to reveal the links between production and consumption—creation and destruction—to integrate societies processes into a sustainable whole.

## CONCLUSION

Today, The Gleaners' Kitchen exists mostly in the æther—in this book and in photos and videos online. But my experience acquiring and sharing food in this way has forever altered the way I look at cooking and the way I look at waste. By sharing food together and actively participating in its production, we can interact with what we are eating in a new and ancient way. Gardening, foraging, Dumpstering, cooking for each other—food production in all its forms—connects us to the grimy source of our food, the dirt from whence it came. Making and sharing food together can cause us to ponder each bite and ask ourselves, "Is this a good thing to put into my body?" If it is, we know it by the way it smells, the way it feels in our hand, and how it tastes in our mouth.

They say that beggars (Dumpster divers?) can't be choosers. In some sense, working with raw ingredients limits choice—copying a specific flavor palate or replicating a takeout dish is almost impossible. But by reducing our freedom to choose somewhat, by choosing to only use simple ingredients, and to cook them with one another, we increase our freedom to create. A single tomato contains a lot of possibilities, and learning what each of those possibilities is can be incredibly liberating. Once ingredients are truly appreciated for what they are, nearly anything can be done with them. And the question "What do I have?" no longer feels so daunting.

This book hints at how to look at the contents of your fridge, and the world around you, through the discerning eyes of a Dumpster diver, even if you would never Dumpster yourself. Everything has a use, and wealth can be found in the most unlikely of places, especially if it's shared. With a little imagination, a trash bin can become a bakery, a back alleyway can be a field of flowers, and the back of your fridge can metamorphose into a banquet fit for you and all your friends. Each ingredient has the ability to transform into something more, to contribute to something greater than the sum of its parts. The value of a meal comes as much from the warm smiles of your friends as it does from the warm fullness in your stomach. Make sure you produce both.

# vegetables

**BOTANICALLY SPEAKING**, a vegetable is any part of an edible plant that isn't the fruit. They come in root form, like carrots and beets; in stem form, like celery and kohlrabi; in leaf form, like kale and lettuce; and even in flower form, like broccoli and artichoke. Foods like zucchini and eggplant are not botanical vegetables because they contain seeds, but most people (and this book) consider them veggies because they need to be cooked. Vegetables are clearly a diverse group of ingredients. One thing that unifies them is the delicate way in which they need to be cooked. Most (but not all) vegetables do need to be cooked before they become edible and tasty, but more than any other food group, vegetables are most easily overcooked, and care should be taken to cook them the minimum amount before eating. Almost every vegetable can be steamed for a couple of minutes and then eaten, but it is usually preferable to stir-fry vegetables in a little bit of oil because that method brings out their flavor. Veggies with low surface area (like beets and not like chard) can be baked in the oven and are usually more resilient to overcooking. The higher the surface area, the more care must be taken not to overcook the food. Vegetables are higher in vitamins, minerals, and fiber than the other ingredient types, but they don't contain that many calories from starch, protein, or fat. A sizable portion of vegetables is essential for any complete meal, but don't count on veggies to make you full. They add texture, flavor, and color, but not much substance. Vegetables are living plant matter, so the fresher they are, the better.

# Artichoke

Artichoke is an edible flower in the thistle family native to the Mediterranean. The artichoke is actually an immature bud of the plant—we eat the base of the petals. If artichoke is allowed to bloom, the petals turn a vibrant lavender.

## STORAGE

· Artichoke should be refrigerated and will keep for about three weeks.

· Artichoke that is brown at the edge of the petals is still edible. Compost it when the whole bud turns brown.

## COOKING

· Artichokes can be **steamed** or **boiled**.

· **Steaming and boiling:** Add artichoke and a few inches of water to a pot and heat for about an hour. The artichoke is done when its color turns an olive green and the outer petals soften and are easily removable.

· **Cook time:** Unlike most vegetables, it is difficult to overcook artichoke, while undercooked artichoke is awful. Make sure to cook artichokes thoroughly.

· Once all the petals are eaten, scrape off the hairs (the "choke" part of the artichoke) to reveal the heart. Artichoke heart tastes like a slightly sweet potato.

## SYNERGIES

· Artichokes can be tasty when served among most other veggies, but it needs to be cooked separately.

· Chop cooked artichoke hearts and mix with spinach and sour cream for your own classic dip.

· A good meal with artichoke will have a heavy protein like meat, beans, or tempeh.

· Artichoke petals are eaten individually. Because of this, it is difficult to add fats and flavorers to an artichoke directly, so a dipping sauce is usually prepared on the side.

· Try making a dip of melted butter and soy sauce, olive oil and lemon, or tomato sauce with sage.

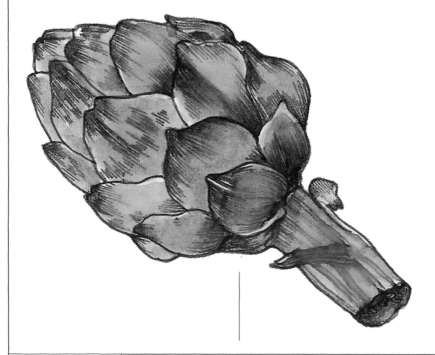

# Asparagus

Asparagus is a grass-like plant native to the Mediterranean. The plant is only edible when it is very immature. The stemmy shoots are cut when they are just emerging out of the ground a few inches, while the leaves are still tiny.

## STORAGE

· Asparagus should be kept refrigerated and will keep for over a week.

· Asparagus tends to go bad from the top and bottom. The tips get slimy and the bottoms become overly fibrous. These bad parts are easy to cut away before cooking the center, which lasts longer.

## COOKING

· Asparagus can be **baked, roasted, steamed**, or **stir-fried**.

· Even if asparagus is quite fresh, its bottoms can be quite tough and fibrous. Cut off the bottom inch before cooking, especially on thicker or older fronds.

· **Cook time:** Asparagus cooks quite quickly, and it is very easy to overcook. The line between crunchy and mushy asparagus is quite thin.

· **Baking** and **stir-frying:** Asparagus browns in oil quite well, whether baked in the oven or stirred in a pan. The asparagus is done in just a few minutes, when the body is soft and the outside is slightly brown and crunchy.

· **Steaming:** Steam asparagus only briefly, so it does not get too mushy.

## SYNERGIES

· Asparagus goes well with most other vegetables but tends to be cooked with ingredients that have similar cook times like broccoli or green beans. Mushrooms can add balance.

· Asparagus can be chopped small and mixed into boiled grains.

· Asparagus goes nicely in stir-fries with tofu or tempeh, and nuts add diversity in texture.

· Asparagus is tasty when slightly sour. Olives, sour citrus, and tomatoes add a nice acidic hint.

· Try making a simple asparagus dish with fresh garlic, lemon, olive oil, and salt.

# Beets

Beets are a root vegetable in the amaranth family native to the Mediterranean. Their leaves are also edible. In fact, cultivars from the same species, *Beta vulgaris*, have been bred for leaf growth and are marketed as chard.

## STORAGE

· Beet roots should be kept refrigerated and will last for over a month.

· As beets age, they will get a bit rubbery. Rubbery beets can still be eaten if they are cooked thoroughly.

· Cut the beet greens away from the root and eat them first. They will only last for a few days, even when refrigerated.

## COOKING BEET ROOTS

· Beets can be **baked, boiled, steamed, roasted, juiced,** or **stir-fried**.

· It is common practice to peel beets before or after cooking, but this isn't necessary. Cooked skins don't taste any different from cooked beet. Just make sure to wash the outside thoroughly before cooking to keep dirt out of your food.

· **Cook time:** Beets are very tolerant to overcooking. Overcooked beets taste fine; they just lose some of their color and crunch. However, undercooked beets are not very palatable. The beet is done when the flesh softens so that it can be cut with a butter knife.

· **Stir-frying:** Beets take longer to stir-fry than just about every other vegetable, so add them first.

· **Boiling and steaming:** After boiling or steaming beets, save the water for soup stock. It is especially useful for boiling grains because it turns them bright pink. Beets are a great soup vegetable.

· Beets have a remarkable red color that will stain everything else you cook them with. Mix them with other food (especially pale foods) as natural food coloring.

## COOKING BEET GREENS

· Beet greens can be **boiled, steamed,** or **stir-fried**.

· **Cook time:** Beet greens cook in just a couple of minutes, but their stems take substantially longer. Take care to cut away the stems and cook them separately first. When beet greens are done, they will be quite soft and will have shrunk down to a fraction of their original size. Turn off the heat once the leaves soften and wilt.

· Beet stems also work as natural food coloring, but the color is not as intense as beet root.

## SYNERGIES

· Beets work well with all vegetables, but pale ones like cauliflower and fennel are great because they take up color well.

· Beets can be roasted with other root veggies or stir-fried with more delicate ones.

· Beets are great mixed in with boiled grains or mashed potatoes, where their color spreads easily.

· Beets can be used as a binder for granola.

· Magenta pesto can be a great addition to pasta. Toss boiled beets in a food processor with some garlic and oil.

· Add a beet or two into chicken soup to make the broth pink.

# Bell Peppers

Bell peppers are the fruit of a shrubby plant in the nightshade family native to Mexico. They are a cultivar of the same species that makes hot chile peppers but have been bred to not produce capsaicin, so they are mild and sweet instead of spicy.

## STORAGE

· Bell peppers should be refrigerated and will keep for about three weeks.

· Bell peppers should be crunchy when prepared. Compost any sections that are mushy or slimy.

## COOKING

· Bell peppers can be **baked, roasted, grilled, stir-fried**, or eaten **raw**.

· Sometimes bell peppers have a secondary fruit, a mini pepper, growing inside them. This is tasty and should not be thrown away!

· Bell peppers come in a variety of colors (green, yellow, orange, and red) and can be mixed raw into almost any dish. Use peppers to add color and vibrancy to your meal.

· **Cook time:** Be careful about overcooking bell peppers. One of the best things about them is their crunch. Some dishes are better with mushy peppers, but make sure you only overcook them deliberately. Bell peppers should only be cooked briefly and are best when warm but essentially raw.

· **Stir-frying:** Only stir-fry bell peppers for a couple of minutes, really just enough time to warm up the flesh without actually cooking.

· **Baking:** Peppers are often baked stuffed with grains and vegetables. They can also be turned into a delicious dip or spread. Bake peppers whole, and when they soften and the outside is slightly crispy, toss them into a food processor with a bit of oil, salt, and other flavorers. The resulting dip will be surprisingly sweet and creamy.

## SYNERGIES

· Raw bell peppers go great in salads with lettuce, cucumber, avocado, tomato, or carrot.

· Try roasting bell peppers, tomatoes, and garlic and then blending them together with some oil and salt to make a rich and creamy tomato sauce.

· Bell pepper strips go great in all kinds of vegetable stir-fries, as well as omelets.

· Cut off the top and use the pepper as a vessel to bake a grain or ground meat stuffing.

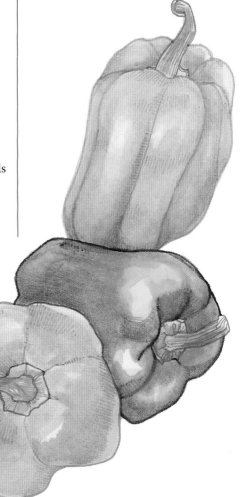

# Broccoli

Broccoli is a member of the Mediterranean species *Brassica oleracea*, along with kale, cauliflower, collard greens, Brussels sprouts, kohlrabi, and cabbage. Broccoli is grown for its dense heads of flower buds, which are eaten before they bloom. The leaves and inner stems are also edible.

### STORAGE

· Broccoli should be refrigerated and will keep for about two weeks.

· Blooming flowers can be eaten. Browning sections of the head can be cut away to preserve the rest.

### COOKING

· Broccoli can be **boiled**, **steamed**, **stir-fried,** or eaten **raw**.

· **Cook time:** Broccoli takes longer to cook than most other delicate vegetables but still cooks rather quickly, in just a few minutes. Broccoli tastes much better when it's still crunchy.

· Broccoli stems are quite tasty, but the outer skin is rather tough. Use a vegetable peeler or paring knife to cut away the green outer skin of the stem. The paler green flesh can be chopped and cooked along with the broccoli and has a similar cook time.

· Broccoli leaves can be cooked like any other leafy green. Take care to remove the fibrous stems before cooking.

### SYNERGIES

· Try chopping up broccoli stems and putting them in a stir-fry with kohlrabi.

· Broccoli can be cooked in big chunks or chopped quite finely and used for soup.

· Broccoli can add a nice crunch to the mushier boiled grains like bulgur wheat.

· Broccoli is often best when cooked simply. Consider tossing it in a pan with a bit of oil, water, salt, and chopped ginger.

# Brussels Sprouts

Brussels sprouts are a member of the Mediterranean species *Brassica oleracea*. They are grown for the densely packed buds that grow at the base of each leaf of the plant.

## STORAGE

· Brussels sprouts are a frost-tolerant plant. They should be kept refrigerated and will keep for over a month.

· Aging Brussels sprout leaves become yellow or brown. These leaves can be peeled away until the bud is green.

## COOKING

· Brussels sprouts can be **baked**, **boiled**, **steamed**, **roasted**, or **stir-fried**.

· Brussels sprouts can be bought on or off the stem. If you get them off the stem, cut off the browning bottom of each bud before cooking.

· **Cook time:** Brussels sprouts take a long time to cook and taste better when they are slightly mushy. Crunchy buds tend to be rather bitter and spicy.

· **Baking:** Bake Brussels sprouts in a deep pan with plenty of oil, water, and flavorers. Cut the large buds in half so that they cook evenly with the smaller buds.

· **Stir-frying:** Cut the buds into small strips so the leaves separate from one another. Stir-fry the leaf strips as you would any other leafy green.

· **Boiling:** Brussels sprouts go nicely in soups. Cut the buds in halves or quarters so they fit easily on a spoon.

## SYNERGIES

· Bake Brussels sprouts and tofu in a deep pan with tons of garlic.

· Brussels sprouts go well with other vegetables that can be cooked for longer time periods, like cabbage, beets, and carrots.

· Try stuffing a turkey with Brussels sprouts and onions.

# Cabbage

Cabbage is a member of the Mediterranean species *Brassica oleracea*. Cabbage leaves grow around each other into a densely packed head that is eaten, but the loose lower leaves are also edible.

## STORAGE

· Cabbage is very cold tolerant. It should be refrigerated and will last for over a month.

· Aging cabbage leaves can wilt and become discolored. These leaves can be peeled away from the cabbage head until fresh leaves cover the exterior.

## COOKING

· Cabbage can be **baked**, **boiled**, **steamed**, **stir-fried**, **roasted**, or **fermented**.

· The cabbage stem where all the leaves attach is usually discarded when the cabbage is chopped, but it is completely edible when cut into small pieces.

· **Cook time:** Cook time varies greatly between cultivars, and unlike other leafy greens, cabbage is usually well cooked when its color fades to slightly brown. Because cook time is so variable, it's good practice to sample a bit of cabbage every once in a while to make sure it cooks to your liking.

· **Baking:** Cut cabbage into quarters and add a lot of water and oil to the bottom of the pan so the leaves don't dry out. When adding flavorers, try to ensure that spices make their way in between the leaves. Cabbage is sometimes baked in vinegar. The vinegar helps break down the fibers that make cabbage so tough.

· **Boiling:** Chopped cabbage goes great in soups.

· **Stir-frying:** Cut the cabbage head into as thin strips as possible. This makes them cook faster and easier to stir in the pan. (It's also quite pretty.)

## FERMENTING

· Many cultures have unique names, like kimchi or sauerkraut, for their particular fermented cabbage dish, but although the details vary, the core fermentation process remains constant. Here's how:

· **Prep:** Chop cabbage and other vegetables with a good crunch into small, bite-size pieces.

· **Salt:** Add a generous amount of salt and mix thoroughly in a bowl. Let the mixture sit for several hours.

· **Flavor:** Add lots of other flavorers.

· **Compress:** Densely pack the mixture and make sure it is fully submerged in liquid.

· **Ferment:** Wait a couple of days or a couple of months for the fermenting bacteria to do their job. Sample the mixture every few days, as it gets stronger, until it is fermented exactly to your liking. Then eat!

# Carrot

Carrot is a root vegetable in the umbel family native to Afghanistan. The carrot life cycle takes two years. In the first year, the plant grows and sends much of its nutrients into the orange taproot to over-winter. At this point, the carrot is usually harvested, but if left alone until spring, nutrients from the taproot are used to produce flowers and seeds.

## STORAGE

· Carrot should be refrigerated and will keep for about a month.

· As carrots age, they become rubbery. Rubbery carrots should not be eaten raw but can be cooked into soups or other dishes where texture is less important.

## COOKING

· Carrots can be eaten **raw** or can be **baked**, **boiled**, **steamed**, **stir-fried**, **juiced**, or **roasted**.

· Carrots are frequently peeled before cooking, but this isn't necessary. Carrot peels taste like carrot.

· **Cook time:** Experiment with how long you cook carrot. Hard and crunchy is nice sometimes, but mushy carrots are great in soups or mashed potatoes. Carrots are one of the few foods where cook time is extremely flexible.

· **Baking** carrots tends to bring out their sweetness more than other cooking methods.

## SYNERGIES

· Shredded or peeled carrot is a great topping on salads.

· Try baking carrots with sweet potatoes and a little bit of honey.

· Steamed carrots can be mashed into potatoes to give the dish orange highlights.

· Carrots can be used as a binder for granola.

· Carrots are nice to add to stir fries with delicate leafy greens. Their orange color adds contrast, and their texture adds a necessary crunch.

# Cauliflower

Cauliflower is a member of the Mediterranean species *Brassica oleracea* grown for its dense heads of teeny flowers, which are eaten before they bloom. The leaves and inner stems are also edible.

## STORAGE

· Cauliflower should be refrigerated and will keep for about three weeks.

· Browning sections of the head can be cut away to preserve the rest.

## COOKING

· Cauliflower can be **boiled**, **steamed**, **roasted**, or **stir-fried**.

· **Cook time:** Let cauliflower cook for a bit longer than you would think. The goal is to have it just a little crunch without being too tough.

· Cauliflower stems are quite tasty, but the outer skin is not. Use a vegetable peeler or paring knife to cut away the harder outer skin. The softer inner flesh can be chopped and cooked along with the cauliflower heads.

· Cauliflower leaves can be cooked like any other leafy green. Take care to remove the fibrous stems before cooking.

## SYNERGIES

· The paleness of cauliflower makes a great palette to experiment with color.

· For purple cauliflower, try boiling it with beets and use red wine instead of water.

· For yellow cauliflower, stir-fry it with some turmeric, along with bell peppers for some extra color.

· Cauliflower has a creaminess about it. It can sometimes be nice cooked with dairy and served as a compliment to a potato dish.

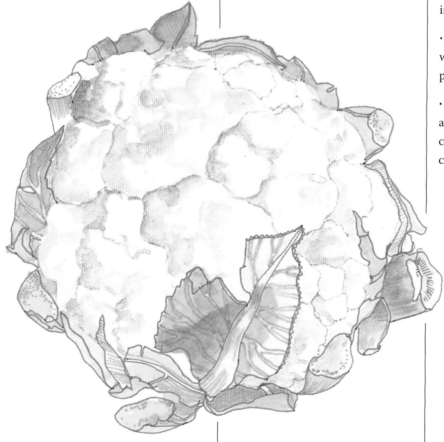

# Celery

Celery is a stem vegetable in the umbel family native to the Mediterranean. Celery is mostly water and fiber, but contrary to popular belief, it does not take more energy to digest celery than you get from eating it.

## STORAGE

· Celery should be refrigerated and will keep for almost a month.

· As celery ages, it becomes rubbery. Rubbery celery should not be eaten raw, but it can be boiled into soups and other dishes where texture is less important.

## COOKING

· Celery is usually eaten **raw**, but it can also be **stir-fried, juiced,** or **boiled** into soup.

· **Cook time:** The most notable quality of celery is its crunch. Celery is crunchiest when raw and softens to mush as it cooks. Choose how crunchy you want your celery to be and cook it accordingly.

· **Boiling:** Celery goes great in soups. If you want crunchy celery in your soup, add it at the end, after the stove is turned off. For mushy celery, add it at the very beginning. Boiling celery for a long time makes it essentially disappear, but it adds a subtle celery flavor to the broth.

· The discarded leaves and stems of celery go great in soup stock.

## SYNERGIES

· Celery is commonly chopped and eaten in salads. It also makes a great base for dips and spreads.

· Try spreading nut butter and dried fruit on a celery stick. (This is called ants on a log.)

· Boil whole bunches of celery with a chicken and then remove the celery bunch before eating to get the celery flavor imbued into the broth without having to worry about the texture.

# Chard

Chard is a leafy vegetable in the amaranth family native to the Mediterranean. Its stems come in many colors from pink to yellow to white. Chard is of the same species as beet, *Beta vulgaris*, but chard is grown for its leaves and beet for its root.

## STORAGE

· Chard should be refrigerated and will only last for a few days.

· Wilted leaves can be cooked, but discolored or slimy leaves should be composted.

## COOKING

· Chard can be **steamed**, **boiled**, or **stir-fried**.

· **Cook time:** Chard cooks very quickly, in just a few minutes. Take care not to overcook it. Chard is finished when the leaves change color to a deep, vibrant green and become very soft.

· When cooked, chard shrinks down to a fraction of its size. Cook more chard than you think you will need.

· Chard stems should be separated from the leaves before cooking because they take significantly longer.

· **Boiling:** When adding chard to soup, add it at the end once the burner is turned off and let the soup sit for a few minutes before serving.

## SYNERGIES

· Chard goes great in omelets. The multicolored leaves add great accent to the eggs.

· Chard can be really wonderful just simply stir-fried alone with some soy sauce and oil. If you don't have enough chard, throw in some other leafy greens.

· Instead of pasta sauce, try mixing chard, garlic, salt, and fresh tomatoes into pasta.

# Collard Greens

Collard greens are a member of the Mediterranean species *Brassica oleracea*. They are grown for their broad leaves, which are flavorful but sometimes tough.

## STORAGE

· Collard greens should be refrigerated and will keep for about a week.

· Slightly yellowing greens are edible when cooked thoroughly, but severely wilted, brown, or slimy leaves should be composted.

## COOKING

· Collard greens can be **boiled**, **steamed**, or **stir-fried**.

· Collard greens are the toughest of the leafy greens commonly sold in supermarkets (tougher than spinach, chard, and kale), but they are still somewhat delicate and easy to overcook.

· **Cook time:** Collards are ready to eat shortly after their color changes to a deep vibrant green. Let them cook for a minute or so after the color changes to make sure the fibers are broken down, but don't let them get too brown.

· When cooked, collard greens shrink down to a fraction of their original size. Cook more than you think you will need.

· Collard stems can be quite fibrous and are usually not eaten unless the leaves are quite young.

## SYNERGIES

· Especially tough collards are sometimes cooked with vinegar. This softens them but also makes them quite pungent.

· Collard greens go great with lots of onions, especially sweet onions.

· Cooked collard greens can be used as a substitute for lettuce in burgers and sandwiches.

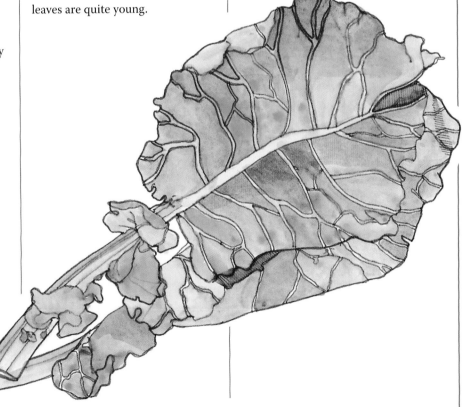

# Eggplant

Eggplant is a vegetable in the nightshade family native to India. The plant is grown for its bulbous purple (and vaguely egg-shaped) fruit, so eggplant is not actually a vegetable in the botanical sense. We call it a vegetable because the fruit must be cooked.

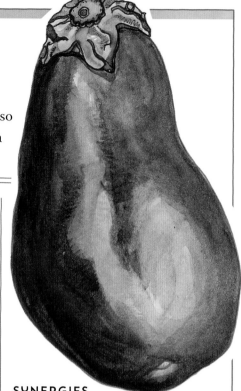

## STORAGE

· Eggplant should be refrigerated and will keep for about three weeks.

· As eggplant ages, its skin will begin to wrinkle, but that doesn't mean the eggplant is going bad. Eggplant is edible as long as its inner flesh is spongy and white.

· Slimy brown spots close to the skin of old eggplant can be cut away and the rest can be salvaged. If the spots dominate the inside of the fruit or if brown streaks are running through it, the entire thing should be discarded.

## COOKING

· Eggplant can be **baked, boiled, grilled, fried, roasted**, or **stir-fried**.

· Eggplant loses a lot of water and shrinks tremendously when cooked. Use more eggplant than you think you will need, especially in stir-fries.

· To reduce the amount of water expelled by eggplant during the cooking process, sprinkle slices with salt and let them sit in a strainer for a couple of hours before cooking. The salt pulls water out of the eggplant via osmosis.

· **Cook time:** Cook time for eggplant is variable, as some like it slightly crunchy and others like it completely dissolved. Eggplant is minimally done when its color changes from white to a pale transparent brown. As it is cooked more, it loses most of its shape and texture, but its flavor generally improves and blends with the other food around it. Experiment with cook times and find what you like best.

· **Baking:** The spongy skin of eggplant is great at absorbing oil. When baking or grilling eggplant, let each slice absorb a sizable amount, but don't let the oil completely permeate (leave some white patches).

· **Boiling:** Eggplant makes a wonderful addition to soups and bean stews. When it is cooked long enough, it basically dissolves into the broth, making it thick and flavorful.

· **Frying:** When frying eggplant, it is usually preferable to coat it first with a mixture of egg, flavorers, and bread crumbs or cornmeal. The coating forms a crispy outer layer and prevents the eggplant inside from absorbing too much oil.

## SYNERGIES

· Baked eggplant goes great in dips. Toss it in a food processor with some flavorers and maybe boiled beans. This is the basis of traditional baba ghanoush and goes great on bread or chips.

· Cooking methods for zucchini and eggplant are quite similar, and they are often cooked together. Try baking a pan of mixed eggplant and zucchini slices with melted cheese on top.

· Boil eggplant with lentils, ginger, and lots of oil to make a rich curry.

· Try making a grilled eggplant and Portobello sandwich. Marinate both in a little bit of oil and other flavorers and then grill them until they shrink and become soft. This is an excellent vegetarian burger substitute.

# Fennel

Fennel is a flavorful vegetable in the umbel family, native to the Mediterranean. The entire plant has a distinctive flavor reminiscent of licorice. Its seeds are commonly used as a spice, and a similar flavor can be captured using the bulbous white stem and green leaves of the plant.

## STORAGE

· Fennel bulbs should be refrigerated and will keep for almost a month.

· Fennel leaves should be separated from the plant and cooked quickly. They will only last a few days, even when refrigerated.

## COOKING

· Fennel can be **baked**, **boiled** into soups, **roasted,** or **stir-fried**.

· **Cook time:** Fennel bulb takes a long time to cook, as it is tastiest when it is quite soft. Fennel is done when the strips of bulb become limp and transparent.

· Fennel leaves and green fennel stalks have different cook times than the bulb. The green portions can actually be eaten raw and require significantly less time when cooked. Cook the green stalks lightly and add the leaves as a garnish once cooking is finished.

· The flavor of fennel can be quite strong, so it is often used as an accent to other vegetables rather than a main ingredient.

## SYNERGIES

· Fennel is a great vegetable to play around with color. Cook fennel with beets or turmeric or both.

· Fennel works particularly well with dairy. Try replacing water with milk when stir-frying or baking fennel and adding a bit of yogurt or cream to fennel soups.

· Fennel greens go great in salad. They add a subtle licorice flavor.

· Add an unusual hint to tomato sauce by baking tomatoes, bell peppers, fennel, and garlic in the oven before blending them with salt, oil, and flavorers.

# Green Beans

Green beans are a cultivar of the common bean (like black beans or kidney beans) that are bred to be harvested while the beans are immature and the surrounding ovaries are still plump with starch.

## STORAGE

· Green beans will keep for about two weeks when refrigerated.

· As green beans age, they develop brown streaks and increase in fibrousness. This is okay; just cut off the brown spots and cook them for longer than normal. However, if the beans grow slimy with soft brown splotches, they should be composted.

## COOKING

· Green beans can be eaten **raw**, or they can be **steamed, stir-fried, grilled**, or **boiled**.

· If green beans are particularly fresh, they should be eaten raw or cooked very minimally (essentially just heated in the pan). As they age, the flesh and the bean within will begin to harden and mature, and they need to be cooked for longer.

· **Cook time:** The average green bean will cook thoroughly in just a few minutes, although cook time varies with bean age. Green beans are finished when their color changes to a deep vibrant green but the flesh is still quite crunchy.

· **Boiling:** When cooking green beans in soup, add them just a few minutes before you take the pot off the stove to ensure they don't overcook.

## SYNERGIES

· Green beans work particularly well with nuts and seeds. Try stir-frying them with butter, soy sauce, and sesame seeds.

· Green beans and asparagus have the same shape, so they mix together quite easily.

· Grating some cheese or sprinkling some nutritional yeast over green beans can make them more filling.

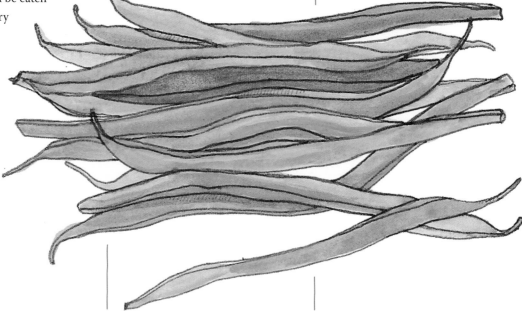

# Kale

Kale is a member of the Mediterranean species *Brassica oleracea*. Kale is grown for its frilly and flavorful leaves. Of all the brassicas, kale leaves are the most delicate.

## STORAGE

· Kale should be refrigerated and will keep for about a week.

· Slightly yellowing greens are edible when cooked thoroughly, but severely wilted, brown, or slimy leaves should be composted.

## COOKING

· Kale can be **boiled**, **steamed**, **stir-fried**, **baked, grilled, juiced**, or eaten **raw**.

· **Cook time:** Kale is ready to eat when its color changes to a deep vibrant green. A pale green color means it is likely undercooked. Slightly brown means it is definitely overcooked. It is extremely easy to overcook kale, so be vigilant.

· Kale stems take longer to cook than the leaves, and some (especially from older, larger plants) are too fibrous to eat at all. Stems should be separated from leaves and cooked for significantly longer.

· **Baking:** To bake kale chips, mix kale, oil, and salt on a baking pan. Bake at a low heat for about half an hour. Kale may need to be stirred occasionally to prevent burning.

· **Raw:** To make a massaged kale salad, mix kale, lemon juice or vinegar, and any flavorings you might want together in a large bowl. The vinegar or lemon juice is necessary because acid is needed to break the chemical bonds that heat usually breaks with other cooking methods. Vigorously squeeze the kale, like you are kneading dough, for about twenty minutes until the color changes to a vibrant green.

## SYNERGIES

· Kale goes great with all vegetables, but it works best with other leafy greens.

· Kale is a nice complement to boiled grains like barley or amaranth.

· Try stir-frying kale with tofu or tempeh, ginger, cumin, and soy sauce.

# Kohlrabi

Kohlrabi is a member of the Mediterranean species *Brassica oleracea*. Kohlrabi is grown for its starchy bulbous stem, but its leaves are also edible.

## STORAGE

· Kohlrabi stems should be refrigerated and will keep for about a month.

· Kohlrabi greens should be separated from the stem and cooked quickly. The greens will keep for about a week when refrigerated.

## COOKING

· Kohlrabi stems can be **boiled, steamed, baked, roasted**, or **stir-fried**.

· Kohlrabi leaves can be cooked like any other leafy green, although they take a while. Be sure to remove the thick fibrous stalks.

· Before cooking kohlrabi stems, make sure to peel away the thick outer skin. The bottom of a kohlrabi stem is quite fibrous, so cut that away too.

· **Cook time:** Kohlrabi is hard and starchy, so it takes longer to cook than most other vegetables. Kohrabi is done when the flesh turns slightly translucent and softens a bit. Take care not to let it get too soft; kohlrabi tastes better when crunchy.

· Kohlrabi stem adds crunch to stir-fries and a slight sweetness to soups.

## SYNERGIES

· Kohlrabi cooks best with other hard and crunchy veggies like carrots, beets, and bell peppers.

· Raw kohlrabi can be a nice addition to salads if it is chopped thinly.

· Kohlrabi can add crunch and texture to pasta dishes.

· Try stewing kohlrabi with beef or pork. The kohlrabi will absorb the flavor of the meat.

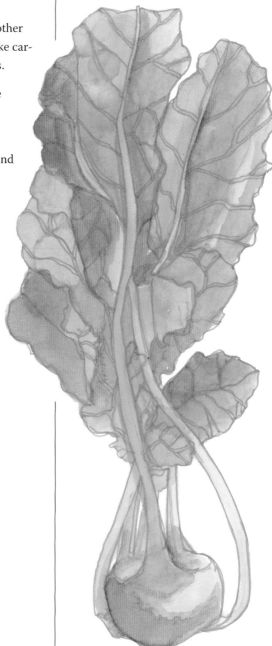

# Lettuce

Lettuce is a delicate leafy vegetable in the sunflower family first domesticated by the ancient Egyptians. Lettuce is harvested when the leaves are still young and bunched together. As the leaves age, they bolt, that is, separate and become filled with bitter latex. Don't eat bolted lettuce!

## STORAGE

· Lettuce spoils quite quickly. Even when refrigerated, it only keeps for a few days. Eat it quick!

## COOKING

· Lettuce should be eaten **raw**.

· Lettuce comes in a variety of shapes, colors, sizes, and flavors. Some are bitter, some are spicy, and some are sweet. All can be eaten raw.

· Lettuce can be added to any dipping sauce or spread that is being blended in a food processor, like pesto or hummus. The lettuce adds bulk and a hint of freshness.

· The ways that lettuce can be prepared are limited, but it is still one of the most utilitarian vegetables. Lettuce can be added on top of just about any dish, adding a good serving of leafy greens with virtually no prep.

## SYNERGIES

· You can mix lettuce into pasta or boiled grains after they've cooked to add some greenness.

· Add nuts or chunks of cheese to lettuce salad to make it more substantial.

· Lettuce can be eaten with other raw leafy greens like spinach or arugula.

## DECORATION

Lettuce is often used for its decorative and aesthetic value. Meat or cheese platters often look much more appealing when they are served on a bed of lettuce. Raw lettuce makes the surrounding food look more fresh.

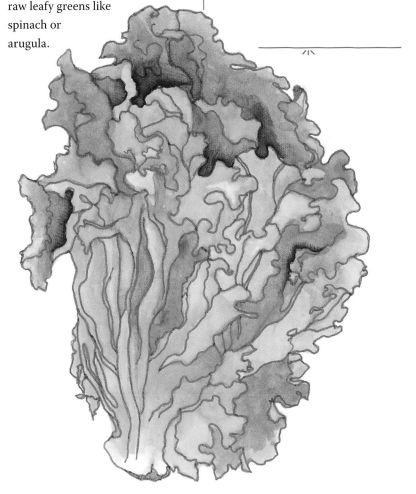

# Mushrooms

Mushrooms are actually fungi, not plants. They are decomposers that grow spongy underground root networks called mycelium that digest buried organic matter. The mushrooms that we eat are actually the fruiting bodies of the fungus—structures similar to flowers that distribute reproductive spores.

### STORAGE

· Mushrooms should be refrigerated and will keep for about two weeks.

· Mushrooms should smell musty and earthy. They should be moist but not slimy. Sour-smelling mushrooms that are slimy with brown splotches should be composted.

### COOKING

· Mushrooms can be **stir-fried**, **grilled**, or **boiled**.

· **Cook time:** Cooking mushrooms takes longer than might be expected, but they are difficult to overcook.

· **Stir-frying:** When cooked, mushrooms release a lot of water and then shrink down to a fraction of their raw size. The released water will dampen your food and imbue it with mushroom flavor.

· **Grilling:** Portobello mushrooms can be grilled and served like burgers.

· **Boiling:** Mushrooms go great in soup—they make the soup more earthy. Mushrooms boiled whole will become juicier and more flavorful with increased cook time.

· Mushrooms have a very distinct flavor but mix well with all sorts of savory food.

### SYNERGIES

· Mushrooms work well in vegetable stir-fries but should be added first because they take longer to cook than delicate greens.

· Mushrooms, onions, and toasted buckwheat make up a traditional eastern European dish called kasha.

· Mushrooms work particularly well with eggs.

· By dry weight, mushrooms, especially the more gourmet species like shiitake or oysters, have a comparable protein content to beans. Consequently, mushrooms make a great meat or bean substitute in vegetarian dishes.

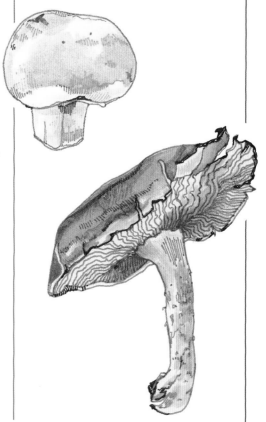

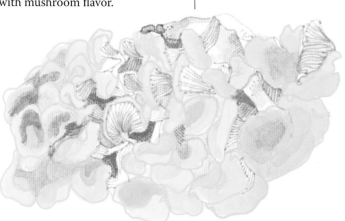

# Okra

Okra is a seed pod vegetable with hybrid origins. There is no known wild ancestor of okra; rather, it is thought that two distinct plant species merged to create the domestic okra plant, which has twice as many genes as any potential ancestor.

### STORAGE

· Okra should be kept refrigerated and will last for over a week.

### COOKING

· Okra can be **steamed**, **stir-fried**, or **boiled** into soup or stew.

· Okra has a mucilaginous texture that it donates to all the other ingredients it's cooked with. Okra slime is great for thickening soups and stews but can be a little off-putting if tasted unexpectedly.

· **Stir-frying:** Stir frying okra whole will keep okras' sliminess isolated inside the seed pods. If okra is sliced before cooking, expect the entire dish to get a bit slippery.

· **Cook time:** Okra cook time varies with personal preference. Some prefer to cook it for just a few minutes, so that it tastes crunchy and the goo stays isolated to just the okra. Others like to stew it for a while, so that the flesh softens and the slime spreads and evens out.

### SYNERGIES

· Okra stir-fries well with other delicate green vegetables like green beans, broccoli, and leafy greens.

· Try pickling okra in diluted apple cider vinegar and salt and then eating it raw.

· Okra works especially well in bean stews with tomato and cheese.

· Gumbo is a traditional Cajun stew heavily featuring okra and tomatoes, usually with beans, shellfish, or chicken as the protein source, and spiced with onions and garlic.

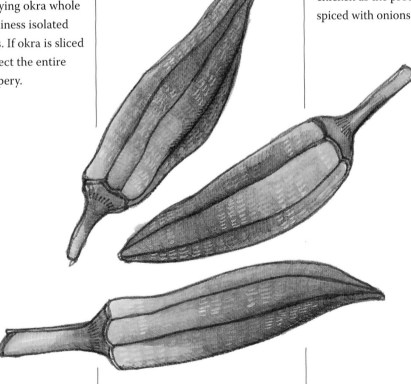

# Radish

Radish is a small root vegetable in the Brassica family first domesticated in Europe. The word *radish* comes from the Latin *radix*, meaning "root." These roots have a great variety of sizes and flavors, like the colossal Japanese daikon and the small Spanish black radish.

## STORAGE

· Radishes should be refrigerated and will keep for over a month.

· As radishes age, they become rubbery. Rubbery radishes are fine to cook with, but don't eat them raw.

## COOKING

· Radishes can be **baked, roasted, stir-fried,** or **boiled** into soup but are most commonly eaten **raw** or **pickled**.

· **Cook time:** Unlike other root vegetables, radishes can actually be quite delicate. They will disintegrate if overcooked. Cook time varies a lot with different radish cultivars. As a rule of thumb, the radish is cooked when its flesh softens and becomes slightly translucent.

· **Pickling:** Pickling can be a complex process that will preserve food for years, but a simple radish pickling can be accomplished in a few minutes. Place radish slices in a small pan or bowl and partially submerge them in vinegar. Add salt and other flavorers and wait for about fifteen minutes for the vinegar to get absorbed. The sour vinegar adds a nice complement to spicier radishes. Radishes pickled in this way will last for several weeks.

## SYNERGIES

· Radish goes well in salads, especially after it's been pickled.

· Boil radish in soups instead of or in addition to potato or other starchy roots. Radish adds starch with a bit more crunch.

· Radish can be sliced and served with dips like hummus, pesto salsa, or even just butter and salt.

# Root Vegetables

Root vegetables are a diverse group of plants grown for their large, edible roots. Most root vegetables are quite strong and flavorful and are usually best suited to be mixed with other ingredients in soups and stews. The milder root vegetables, carrots and beets, have been given their own sections because they are more frequently cooked on their own.

### STORAGE

· Root vegetables should be refrigerated and will keep for over a month.

· As root vegetables age, they get a bit rubbery. Rubbery roots can still be eaten as long as they are cooked thoroughly.

### COOKING

· Root vegetables can be **stir-fried, fried, roasted,** or **baked**, but the best way to cook them is usually to **boil** them in soups or stews.

· Some root vegetables (like celeriac) have particularly thick skins and gnarled, knobby surfaces. For these vegetables, peel or cut the skin away before cooking. Roots with thinner skins do not need to be peeled.

· **Cook time:** All root vegetables should be cooked for a long time. They contain lots of starch and fiber and need to be exposed to heat for a long time to convert those starches and fibers to tasty sugars. Root vegetables aren't done until their flesh is quite soft and can be cut with a spoon.

· **Baking:** Baking root vegetables tends to bring out their sweetness. The dry heat breaks down starch into sugar but unlike boiling, keeps the sugars contained in the flesh.

· **Boiling:** Boiling root vegetables is often preferable because boiling allows the flavor of the stronger ones, like parsnip and celeriac, to permeate the water.

· **Frying:** Root vegetables can be fried just like potatoes. Cut them into a French fry shape and fry them in a pan with a modest amount of oil. They taste quite similar to fried potatoes, but sweeter and more like a vegetable.

### SYNERGIES

· Root vegetables can be boiled with potatoes and mashed together to add some diversity of flavor to the potatoes.

· Because root vegetables have to be cooked for so long in order to be tasty, it's nice to serve them alongside raw or briefly cooked vegetables like bell peppers or leafy greens to keep the meal feeling fresh.

· Root vegetables add an essential element to the flavor of stews made from meat or beans.

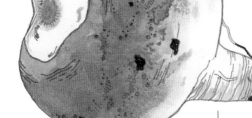

# Spinach

Spinach is a small and delicate leafy vegetable in the amaranth family, native to the Middle East. It has one of the highest vitamin and mineral contents of all veggies. It can be eaten raw, so it's great when you're in a rush.

## STORAGE

· Spinach spoils extremely quickly. Even when refrigerated, it only lasts a few days.

· Spinach that is even slightly slimy should be composted.

## COOKING

· Spinach can be eaten **raw**, but it can also be **steamed**, **boiled**, **stir-fried**, or **juiced**.

· **Cook time:** Spinach cooks extremely quickly, in about a minute. Spinach is thoroughly cooked as soon as (or even before) the leaves wilt and lose their form. Be careful not to overcook it. Overcooked spinach tastes bad and destroys many important nutrients.

· When spinach cooks, it shrinks tremendously. Add more spinach to the pot than you think you will need.

· Spinach breaks down so completely that it is often shredded and added to dips and bread spreads.

· **Raw:** Raw spinach is great on its own or in salads. Raw spinach can also be used in conjunction with basil in pesto to add more bulk without sacrificing flavor.

· **Boiling:** Spinach makes a great addition to the end of soups because it cooks so quickly. Mix a handful or two of spinach into the pot once the stove is turned off.

## SYNERGIES

· Spinach goes really great with mushrooms and scrambled eggs.

· Try making a spinach salad with fresh tomatoes, shredded carrot, sunflower seeds, and cheese.

· Mix raw spinach into freshly strained pasta. The heat from the pasta will cook it just enough to stay slightly crunchy.

# Zucchini

Zucchini is a squash native to Mexico. The identifiable form and flavor of zucchini was developed by Italian farmers in the 1800s. Zucchini is usually harvested while the fruit is small and immature, as larger zucchinis tend to be bland and fibrous.

## STORAGE

· Zucchini will keep for about two weeks when refrigerated.

· When zucchini is being prepared for cooking, it should be crunchy and its flesh should be white. Brown portions should be composted.

## COOKING

· Zucchini can be **baked**, **grilled**, **roasted**, **stir-fried**, **boiled** into soups, or **fried**.

· Before cooking zucchini, it is sometimes helpful to sprinkle salt on the slices and let them sit in a strainer for a couple of hours. The salt pulls water out of the zucchini via osmosis, which makes it taste less bland. This trick is especially helpful with very large garden zucchini whose bulk is mostly excess water.

· **Cook time:** In general, zucchini is done when it softens slightly, although how soft is a matter of taste. Be careful not to let zucchini become too mushy.

· **Baking:** Baked zucchini is done when it is slightly brown and crispy, usually in about half an hour.

· **Stir-frying:** Experiment with oil levels when cooking zucchini. Using a lot of oil in stir-fries browns the slices nicely and gives them a fuller flavor, but it is sometimes also nice to use little or no oil, which leaves the zucchini lighter and tasting more green.

· **Frying:** When frying zucchini, consider coating the slices with flour or cornmeal, egg, and spices. The coating makes a crunchy crust when fried and prevents the zucchini from absorbing too much oil.

## SYNERGIES

· Cooking methods for eggplant and zucchini are quite similar, and they are often cooked together. Try baking them together with some pepper and cheese sprinkled on top.

· Baked or boiled zucchini is a great addition to tomato sauce.

· Try frying zucchini with tofu and cardamom seeds.

· Overly large zucchini are great for baking into zucchini bread or can be used as a binder in granola.

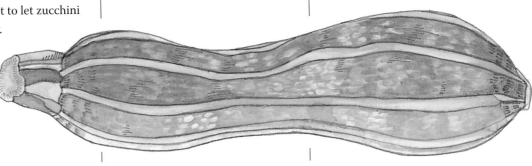

# Squash

Squashes and gourds are a group of large, ground-dwelling plants with broad leaves and very large fruit. They are native to Mexico, where they were first cultivated by Native Americans as part of the famous "three sisters": corn, beans, and squash.

**Butternut squash** is the sweetest of the common squashes and does well with a sweet palate.

**Acorn squash** has ridges that make it difficult to peel, so it is often cut in half and baked. The easiest way to peel it for soup is to cut it into sections defined by the ridges and peel each section separately.

**Spaghetti squash** should not be steamed. When it is baked, the flesh breaks up into spaghetti-like tendrils that are fun to eat.

**Pumpkins** are larger, more fibrous, and blander than other squash varieties, which is why they are often used decoratively rather than for cooking. Pumpkins can be cooked, but they require longer cook times and extra flavorers.

## STORAGE

· Squash can be stored unrefrigerated for about a month.

· When squash goes bad, the sides get mushy and the skin cracks. If you notice a mushy spot, cut it off and refrigerate the squash or cook it right away. If you catch rot early, most of the squash can be salvaged.

## COOKING

· Squash can be **boiled**, **steamed**, or **baked**. Boiling squash is quicker and easier than baking (as there is no risk of burning or overcooking), but baking tends to bring out better flavors.

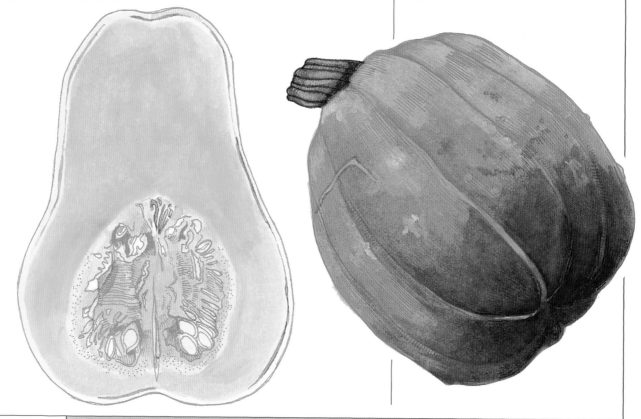

- **Cook time:** Squash takes quite a long time to cook. Steaming is significantly faster than baking but still takes at least half an hour. Squash is done when its color becomes more vivid and the flesh can be easily scooped with a spoon.

- **Baking:** Squash should be baked whole, and baking can take over an hour in some cases. It is a good idea to add oil or water or both to baking squash to make sure it stays moist. If you are not adding flavorers, baking squash facedown also prevents the flesh from drying out.

- **Boiling:** Boiled squash makes an excellent base for soups. Squash chunks can be left in the soup whole, or they can be blended with an immersion blender to give the entire soup a rich, creamy texture.

## SYNERGIES

- Squash is one of the few ingredients that goes well in both sweet and savory dishes. Its synergies are diverse.

- Yogurt can be nice as a topping on baked squash. It adds coolness and moisture and balances out the flavor.

- Baked squash can be served alongside other bakeable foods like sweet potato, carrots, or beets. It's good to also serve it with something like fresh leafy greens for textural diversity.

- Squash can add a richness and sweetness to the broths of chicken or lentil soup.

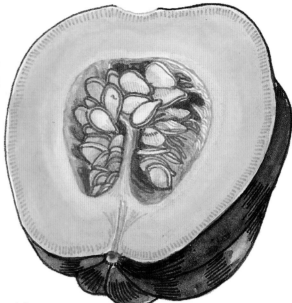

### BAKING SQUASH SEEDS

Squash seeds can be baked in the oven for a tasty snack. They are crunchy and high in protein. Here's how to bake squash seeds:

- Remove the seeds and clean off any residue with water.

- Put them in a baking pan with a very generous amount of oil, salt, and other flavorers like garlic, turmeric, or pepper.

- Bake on a medium heat for over an hour.

- Take the seeds out periodically to make sure they cook evenly.

- The seeds are done when they turn golden brown and puff up a little bit.

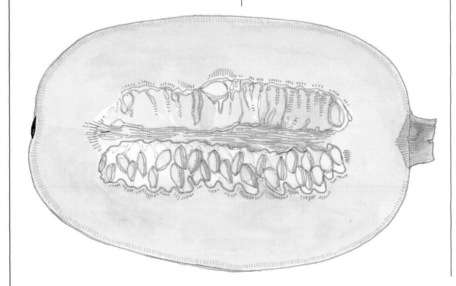

# carbohydrates

●┼┼┼┼┼┼┼┼┼●

**HUMANS RELY ON CARBOHYDRATES** more than any other food type to give us the calories we need to live. Most carbohydrates come from a family of grasses known as cereals. The cereals were the first plants to be domesticated by humans, and their oversized seeds are called *grains*. Domestication of grains was a monumental achievement in human history—it marks the transition from hunter-gatherer to agricultural societies. Society's most important carbohydrates—wheat, rice, and corn—are all cereal grains, but many important carbohydrate sources—notably potato, plantain, and cassava—are not seeds at all. Regardless of their botanical origins, all carbohydrates are packed with starch (that is, sugar) and fiber but don't have much in the way of vitamins and minerals. They provide a reliable source of energy to get you through the day but don't provide much nutritional value. Creative cooks can process grain seeds into unusual forms, like bread and pasta, because of a binding protein many cereals contain called gluten. In the absence of these processing methods, the standard way to cook any grain is simply to boil it. Many cookbooks will dictate specific water-to-grain ratios for boiling each grain, but a simple rule of thumb works just as well: cover the grain with water deep enough to submerge your thumbnail. When you boil a grain, it absorbs water, softens, and becomes ready to eat. Carbohydrates have formed the backbone of the human diet throughout our history, and no meal is complete without a generous serving.

# Amaranth

Amaranth is a diverse group of plant species native to Central America. Some amaranths are cultivated as a leafy green, but it is most commonly eaten as a grain. Amaranth is not a true grain, as it does not come from a cereal grass. Amaranth has a higher protein content than most grains.

## STORAGE

· Amaranth can be stored unrefrigerated in a dry place for several years.

## COOKING

· **Cook time:** The best way to cook amaranth is to **boil** it. Amaranth boils very quickly.

· **Boiling:** Cover amaranth with water deep enough to submerge your thumbnail and cook until the water is absorbed and the amaranth is soft. Add more water if necessary.

· Boil amaranth in vegetable stock for extra flavor.

· Amaranth grains are small and rubbery and resemble caviar. When cooked, they tend to clump together, giving them a unique texture for a boiled grain.

· Amaranth can be eaten alone, boiled into soup, or mixed into a stir-fry.

## SYNERGIES

· Try boiling amaranth with nuts or seeds, which can complement amaranth's already-chewy texture.

· Amaranth can be boiled directly with mushrooms, beets, or carrots.

· Cheese can make amaranth clump together even more than it already does.

· Mixing amaranth and corn meal and boiling them together will make a polenta with a bit of crunch.

· Amaranth can make a nice hot breakfast cereal, as a substitute to oatmeal. Try boiling it with some milk, honey, and dried fruit.

### POPPING

Amaranth can be popped like popcorn. Here's how:

· Place a thick-bottomed pot on a high heat with just the tiniest amount of high-temperature oil and leave it there for several minutes.

· Once the pot gets very hot, pour enough amaranth into the pot to cover it with a single layer of seeds.

· Stir the seeds with a large spoon for a few seconds until they pop. Be careful not to burn them!

· Popped amaranth is a great topping on salads and stir fries or sprinkled on yogurt. It adds a nice fluffy crunch. It can be eaten as a snack like popcorn or used instead of breadcrumbs for fried dishes.

# Barley

Barley is a cereal grain native to the Middle East. The Old English word for barley was *bære*, which unsurprisingly bears a strong resemblance to the modern word *beer*. Barley beer was likely fermented into one of humanity's first alcoholic beverages.

## STORAGE

· Barley can be stored unrefrigerated in a dry place for several years.

## COOKING

· **Cook time:** The best way to cook barley is to **boil** it. Barley is a large grain and takes longer than most grains to cook.

· **Boiling:** To boil barley, cover it with water deep enough to submerge your thumbnail and cook until the water is absorbed and the barley is soft. Add more water if necessary. Putting a lid on the pot helps conserve heat and water.

· Boil barley in vegetable stock for extra flavor.

· Barley grains are quite large and chewy—expect a consistency more similar to noodles than porridge.

· Barley can be eaten alone, boiled into soup, or mixed into a stir-fry. Barley flour also makes excellent bread.

## SYNERGIES

· Barley is a great addition to chicken soup because the large seeds can be boiled for quite a long time before getting overly mushy.

· Try chopping up green vegetables like okra, green beans, or asparagus and mixing them into cooked barley.

· Cheese or nutritional yeast can add weight to barley.

## SPROUTING

· Soak whole barley grains in water for a few days and the seeds will begin to grow and sprout.

· The sprouting process begins to break down the dense grain, so sprouted barely is great for those with gluten sensitivity.

· Sprouted barely can be boiled and used like any other grain (although it boils much more quickly).

· Barley sprouts can also be baked in bread, where it will make the bread taste richer and heartier.

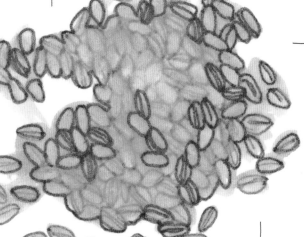

# Flour and Sourdough

Flour is made from ground grains. In antiquity, bits of grass were inevitably harvested with the grain and grinding everything into flour was a good way to process those impurities. Today, our harvesting and processing methods are more sophisticated, and the use of flour has evolved into an art form. However, one of the earliest fermentation methods, sourdough, is still one of the most popular.

## COOKING WITH FLOUR

· Flour makes a great thickener for soups and sauces. Mix a few spoonfuls of flour into soup and it will dissolve and make the broth richer, heavier, creamier, and milder.

· Flour is often baked unfermented into pies, cookies, cupcakes, muffins, and other pastries. In these cases, baking soda is used as a leavening agent instead of yeast.

· A frying batter can be made with eggs, flour, and flavorers. Mix the three together and coat them over your food to be fried. The batter will absorb the fry oil and make a crunchy exterior while the food on the inside cooks evenly but doesn't get too oily.

## FERMENTING SOURDOUGH

· Make a watery mixture of flour and water in a bowl. It should be more watery than normal dough.

· You can add sugar or a pinch of yeast to speed up the fermentation process, or you can leave the mixture alone for a wild fermentation. Store-bought yeast is faster and more reliable, but wild yeast has a more distinct flavor.

· Let the mixture sit out for about a week. Once you are sure there is yeast fermenting the mixture, you should probably cover it with a cloth to prevent further contamination.

· After about a week, the mixture will smell very pungent and bready. Add it to a large mixing bowl along with plenty more flour and water and mix them together into dough.

· It's often nice to add sprouted whole grains like barley, wheat or rye to the sourdough.

· Knead the dough and then let it rise and ferment overnight. Take a portion of this dough and put it back into your original bowl with some more water and flour or sprouted grains. This will be your sourdough starter for next time.

· Bake the rest of the dough in the oven. Eat it fresh! Freshly baked bread with some butter is one of life's great joys.

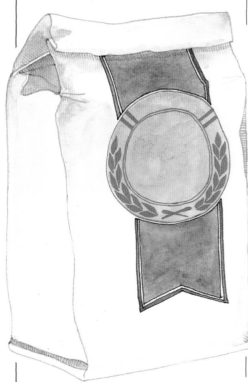

# Bread

Bread is one of the most ancient foods eaten by humans and is made by fermenting dough with yeast. The yeast breaks down starch, producing bubbles of carbon dioxide, which makes the dough rise. A protein in wheat called gluten keeps the dough bound together, so that the carbon dioxide bubbles expand the dough but don't break it. The dough is baked in a large oven and eaten.

### BREAD STORAGE

· Bread goes stale quite quickly, in under a day, if left out in the open air. Even if kept in sealed plastic or in a bread box, bread will go stale in just a few days.

· Bread stored at room temperature will grow mold in about a week. Mold can be white, green, or black. Moldy bread should be composted.

· Bread can be frozen and will keep for several months. Stale or frozen bread can be revived by heating it in a toaster or oven.

### COOKING WITH BREAD

· Bread is best when fresh or toasted with a little bit of butter. Most of the cooking methods involving bread are strategies to deal with stale bread.

· Bread can be toasted into crackers. Put slices on a low heat in the oven for about half an hour until they are very crispy. Break the toasted slices up into cracker-size pieces, or even smaller to make croutons, or mix them in a food processor to make bread crumbs.

· Coat food in a mixture of egg and bread crumbs before frying. The bread crumbs make the outside crunchy while keeping the inside moist.

· Bread can be baked into casseroles or boiled into stew. Break up bite-size chunks and mix them in with the vegetables and protein. The bread will absorb water and add a creamy starchiness somewhat similar to potato.

· Bread can be made into French toast. Soak the bread slices in a mixture of beaten egg, milk or cream, and sweet spices like cinnamon, nutmeg, and clove. Cook the slices in a frying pan with butter. Each side is done when it turns golden brown.

### SYNERGIES

· Bread is perhaps the most important carbohydrate in a Western diet, and it can be eaten with virtually everything.

· Countless spreads, both sweet and savory, are commonly put on bread, such as nut butters, guacamole, fruit compote, hummus, pesto, salsa, jelly, jam, or aioli.

· Bread goes particularly well with high-protein foods like eggs, cheese, and meat.

· Bread is a key complement to most soups, where it adds balance and absorbs excess broth.

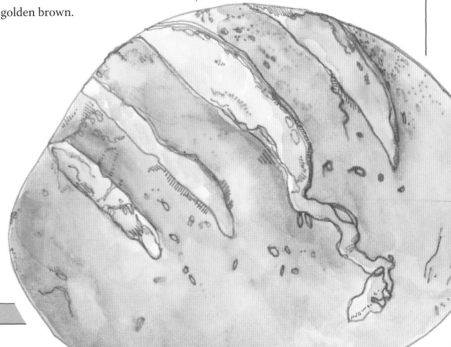

# Buckwheat

Buckwheat is the seed of a small ground shrub native to Southeast Asia. Buckwheat is not as productive as the cereal grains, but it is an essential crop in colder regions where the growing season is short.

## STORAGE

· Buckwheat can be stored unrefrigerated in a dry place for several years.

## COOKING

· Buckwheat has a distinctly nutty flavor that should be highlighted by **toasting** the seeds before **boiling** them.

· **Toasting:** To toast buckwheat seeds, put them in a large frying pan with a little bit of oil and mix them on high heat. In a few minutes, the room should fill with a distinct buckwheat fragrance. Toast the seeds until they darken significantly, but be careful not to burn them. Proper toasting is essential to ensure that the seeds don't break apart into mush when you boil them.

· **Boiling:** As the seeds are toasting, boil water in a separate pot. Once buckwheat is toasted, pour enough boiling water over the seeds to submerge them in the pan. Cook time is very short. Boiling is done when all the water is absorbed and the buckwheat is soft and puffy.

· Boil buckwheat in vegetable stock for extra flavor.

## SYNERGIES

· Buckwheat is often considered a winter food and cooked with hearty vegetables like cabbage or squash. However, it's nice to serve it alongside asparagus or fresh leafy greens.

· Try serving buckwheat with tempeh and nuts. The "earthy" flavors all complement each other.

· It's good to use a lot of flavorful vegetables when cooking buckwheat—onions, garlic, and maybe even horseradish.

· Mushrooms, onions, and toasted buckwheat make up a traditional eastern European dish called kasha.

# Bulgur Wheat

Wheat is a highly productive cereal grain native to the Middle East. While wheat is most commonly ground into flour, its loose grains are often cut and boiled as bulgur wheat.

### STORAGE

· Bulgur wheat can be stored unrefrigerated in a dry place for several years.

### COOKING

· Bulgur wheat is best when **boiled**. It comes to market partially boiled already, so it requires less water than other cereal grains.

· **Boiling (sort of):** Rather than boiling bulgur wheat in water, it is often easier to pour already-boiling water over the bulgur grains.

Pour in enough boiling water to slightly cover the grains and then wait for about half an hour for the grains to absorb the water.

· Boil bulgur wheat in vegetable stock for extra flavor.

· Bulgur wheat is best when served warm, but it is popular to make bulgur salads out of vegetables and cold bulgur.

### SYNERGIES

· Bulgur wheat requires minimal cooking, so it's good to serve it with vegetables that also don't need to be cooked much, like celery, carrots, or spinach.

· Bulgur is a great side to bean dishes. It is also nice to add nuts or seeds.

· Try adding fresh tomatoes or olives to a cold bulgur salad.

# Corn

Corn is a cereal grain native to Mexico. It is the most heavily modified of all the domesticated cereals. An ear of corn bears almost no resemblance to the small grass from which it originated. Today, corn is the most widely cultivated crop in the world. Corn has many nonculinary uses, but the most common forms of edbile corn are corn on the cob, popping corn, cornmeal, and cornstarch.

### CORN ON THE COB

Corn on the cob is usually the only form of corn people associate with the plant. Because of its large size and bright colors, people often consider corn on the cob a vegetable, but from a nutritional perspective, it should be thought of as a carbohydrate.

### COOKING CORN ON THE COB

· Corn on the cob can be **boiled** or **grilled**.

· **Cook time:** Corn on the cob barely needs to be cooked at all, especially if it is fresh. Cook corn on the cob basically until it gets hot and not much longer.

· **Boiling:** To boil corn on the cob, remove the husk and then place it in boiling water for a few minutes. The corn is cooked when it becomes slightly more vibrant and yellow.

· **Grilling:** To grill corn on cob, put it on a grill or open flame with the husk still on. The husk will smoke and burn. Remove the corn after a few minutes before the flame burns all the way through the husk.

· **Corn off the cob:** Corn kernels can be cut off the cob before cooking and then tossed into soups or stir-fries. This is a useful trick to save corn ears that are going bad.

### POPCORN

Popcorn can be bought in microwave packages, but it is easy and much tastier to pop it yourself. The simplest way to make popcorn is with a large soup pot.

### MAKING POPCORN

· Fill the bottom of the pot with about one layer of popcorn kernels and a little bit of oil.

· Place the pot, with a lid, on the stove on high heat.

· While the pot is heating, intermittently shake it to move the kernels around. Shake the pot at least once a minute.

· After a few minutes the kernels will begin to pop. Continue to heat the pot and shake it vigorously for a couple of minutes.

· Turn the heat off and let the pot sit for a bit while the last kernels pop.

### SYNERGIES

· Try using spreads other than butter on corn on the cob. Pesto, hummus, and salsa all are surprisingly tasty.

· Nutritional yeast and paprika are fantastic flavorers for popcorn. They add weight, zing, and rich colors.

# Cornmeal and Cornstarch

Much of the world's industrially grown corn is ground and cooked into other food products. Cornmeal is coarsely ground corn kernels, and cornstarch is finely ground corn kernels.

## CORNMEAL

Cornmeal is made by partially grinding dried corn kernels. It can be eaten on its own as a grain or baked into breads and pastries.

· **Boiling:** Cornmeal can be boiled with flavorers into polenta. Add enough water to just barely cover the cornmeal. Unlike other boiled grains, polenta forms a solid mass that can be molded into different shapes.

· Corn grits are made by boiling cornmeal in excess water, resulting in a kind of porridge.

· **Frying:** A frying batter can be made with eggs, cornmeal, and flavorers. Mix the three together and coat them over your food to be fried. The batter will absorb the fry oil and make a crunchy exterior, while the food on the inside cooks evenly but doesn't get too oily.

## SYNERGIES

· Simple polenta can be made more interesting by baking it in the oven with other ingredients after it's been boiled. Try making a layered casserole with polenta, tomatoes, cheese, and thinly sliced meat.

· Cornmeal boiled into grits can be either sweet or savory. Grits go well with salt and cheese or with milk and fruit.

## CORNSTARCH

Cornstarch is made by grinding dried corn kernels into a fine powder. Cornstarch is often used by industrial food processors as a cheap thickener.

· **Thickening:** Mix a few spoonfuls of cornstarch into hot soup or sauce and it will dissolve and make the broth richer, heavier, creamier, and milder.

· Cornstarch can be used as a glue instead of a food. Boil a mixture of cornstarch and water for about half an hour until it turns into a thick, semitransparent, sticky fluid. Vary the ratio of water to cornstarch to alter the balance between stickiness and fluidity. Wait for it to cool and then use it in generous amounts as an adhesive for paper. Before boiling, this mixture forms a fascinating non-Newtonian fluid called oobleck, which is a great and messy toy.

# Millet

Millet is a sort of catchall name for large number of cereal grains with diverse evolutionary origins. Millets are usually more drought tolerant and can thrive in poorer soil than the highly domesticated grains like corn, rice, and wheat, but their yields are correspondingly poorer. Most global millet production occurs in developing nations.

## STORAGE

· Millets can be stored unrefrigerated in a dry place for several years.

## COOKING

· **Cook time:** The best way to cook millet is to **boil** it. Millet boils quite quickly.

· **Boiling:** Cover millet with water deep enough to submerge your thumbnail and cook until the water is absorbed and the millet is soft. Add more water if necessary.

· Boil millet in vegetable stock for extra flavor.

· **Toasting:** Millet is often toasted before cooking to enhance its nutty flavor. To toast millet, heat it in a pan with a bit of oil for a few minutes before you boil it.

· Leftover millet sticks together quite nicely and can be shaped into patties and fried like a veggie burger or potato pancakes.

· Millet grasses are closely related to corn. Millet seeds have a similar texture and flavor to cornmeal but are more fluffy, crumbly, and earthy.

## SYNERGIES

· Add some crunch to a millet dish by mixing in bits of fennel or kohlrabi.

· Crack an egg or melt some cheese into millet to help it stick together and add some weight.

· Millet can be eaten as a breakfast cereal. Heat it with milk, nuts, and dried fruit.

· Mix millet with cornmeal to make polenta or grits that are a bit nuttier and more brittle.

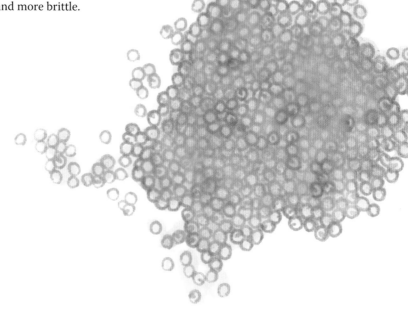

# Noodles

Noodles are made by extruding a mixture of flour and water into a desired shape and then drying it for several hours. Thousands of shapes are produced, and many different kinds of flours are used, most commonly wheat and rice flour. Traditional Italian pasta is made using durum wheat, which is particularly dense and high in protein.

### STORAGE

· Dried noodles can be stored unrefrigerated for several years.

· Fresh pasta like ravioli, tortellini, or gnocchi must be refrigerated or frozen.

### COOKING

· All noodles must be **boiled** before serving.

· **Cook time:** Noodles come in a huge variety of shapes and sizes, and cook time varies greatly but will usually be under fifteen minutes.

· Boil noodles for shorter times than you might expect. It is extremely easy to overcook noodles, especially those made with rice flour. Noodles are best when they are just a little bit crunchy.

· Once boiled, noodles are usually eaten with a variety of sauces, but they can also be added to stir-fries, added to soups, baked into a casserole (think lasagna), or chilled and mixed with vegetables (pasta salad).

· When storing noodle soups, be sure to separate the noodles from the broth so that they don't disintegrate.

### SYNERGIES

· Cut vegetables small and mix them into the pasta once it is done cooking. Leafy greens and fresh tomatoes work especially well.

· Cheese can be melted into pasta by heating them together on the stove, or it can be sprinkled on top before serving.

· Meat or tempeh chunks mix with pasta beautifully. Nuts add a nice crunch.

· Don't be afraid to add a generous amount of fat to pasta dishes. Pasta tastes bland without butter or oil.

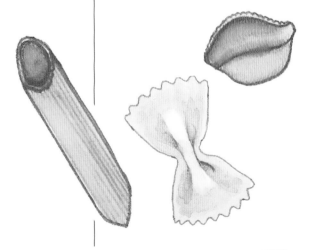

# Oats

Oats are a cereal grain native to the Middle East. Like other grains, oats grow with a thick hull that makes them difficult to eat. This hull is removed by a unique process that involves rolling the oats flat. The hull can also be removed by cutting the oats in half—hence rolled oats and steel-cut oats.

## STORAGE

· Oats can be stored in a dry place unrefrigerated for several years.

## COOKING

· Oats can be **boiled** into oatmeal or **baked** into granola.

### OATMEAL

· To boil oatmeal, heat oats in a pan with enough water to just barely submerge the oats. Milk can be used instead of water to make the oatmeal richer and creamier.

· Fruit, nuts, yogurt, cinnamon, and sweeteners are all nice additions.

· **Cook time:** Oatmeal cooks quickly and is done when all the excess liquid is absorbed.

### GRANOLA

· Use a cheese grater or food processor to shred apples, zucchini, beets, or carrots. The shredded plant matter acts as a binder and helps form granola clusters.

· Mix oats, sweeteners, and a fruit/vegetable binder in a pan. The sweeteners also help to bind the granola together, so be generous.

· **Cook time:** Bake the mixture in the oven at a low heat for an hour or two. It is very important to take the

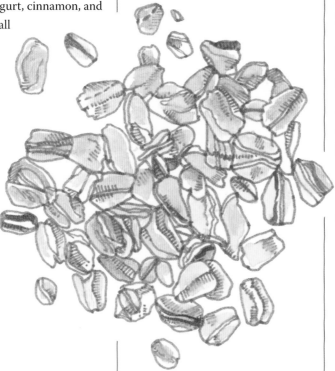

oats out of the oven and stir them every 20 minutes or so to ensure that cooking is even and nothing burns.

· It's nice to add nuts, fresh fruit, dry fruit, or spices like cinnamon, clove, or nutmeg. Make sure to add dry fruit after baking because dried fruits should be eaten raw and do not bake well.

## SYNERGIES

· In addition to carrots, beets, zucchini, and apples, plaintain can be used as a very effective and sweet binder for granola.

· Nuts are an essential component in most oat dishes. They greatly improve the texture.

· Oats work well with just about every kind of fruit, even exotic ones like papaya or kiwi.

· Milk, yogurt, or cream can be used pretty much interchangeably with oats.

# Plantain

Plantain is a seedless, sterile hybrid fruit of two different species of broad-leaved, tropical plants native to Southeast Asia. There is no dramatic genetic distinction between plantains and bananas, which are also hybrids of the same two species. Plantains are more fibrous and starchy than bananas and need to be cooked.

## STORAGE

· Plantains can be stored unrefrigerated for about two weeks.

· Plantains can be eaten at all stages of ripeness, from green to yellow to black. Most people prefer to cook them when they are yellow with black spots. Black plantains are still edible but are very mushy and difficult to cook with.

## COOKING

· Plantains can be **baked**, **fried**, **steamed**, **grilled**, **roasted**, or **boiled**.

· **Cook time:** Green plantains are quite hard and starchy and may be difficult to peel. They need to be cooked extensively to convert the starches into sugar and will taste similar to potato. As plantains ripen, they become softer, fruitier, and sweeter and require less cook time.

· **Baking:** To bake a plantain, peel it, cut it into disks, and place it on a baking pan with a little bit of oil. Put it in the oven on medium heat. Cook time will be about half an hour and will vary with ripeness. When the plantain is finished, it will be quite soft and golden brown.

· **Frying:** To fry plantains, add about a half inch (1 cm) of high-temperature oil to a frying pan and heat on high for a few minutes. Add peeled and cut plantain disks to the oil once it is hot—be careful not to let the oil splash. Flip the plantains once the edges begin to brown (in five or ten minutes depending on ripeness). It may be necessary to reduce the stove heat to prevent burning. Well-fried plantain will be crispy on the outside and soft on the inside.

· **Stir-frying:** It is possible to stir-fry plantains with much less oil—but this is difficult because less oil means more stirring, and excessive stirring destroys the plantain.

· **Steaming and boiling:** Steamed plantain is quite mushy but requires no oil.

· A plantain's flavor palate depends on its ripeness. Green plantains will be starchy and go well with flavoring vegetables like onions and garlic. Ripe plantains will be fruitier and go well with sweeteners and cinnamon.

## SYNERGIES

· Squash and plantain have surprisingly similar flavor palates. Both are slightly sweet but can be eaten in either sweet or savory dishes.

· Plantain can be baked with other kinds of fruit, like apples or pears, to make a sweet and starchy dessert.

· Yogurt is a fantastic condiment for fried plantain. It adds a cool creaminess. Try mixing a bit of chopped mint into the yogurt and use it as a dipping sauce.

# Potato

Potatoes are a tuber from a plant in the nightshade family, native to the Andes Mountains in Peru. As a tuber, potatoes are formed from the bud of a stem that grows downward and submerges itself in the earth. The plant enlarges the bud with starch until a potato tuber is produced. Look closely at a potato, and you will find tiny leaf scars from the bud.

## STORAGE

· Potatoes can be stored unrefrigerated for about three weeks and longer in the fridge.

· Rotting potatoes will become mushy and slimy and should be composted. If the rot is caught early enough, it can be cut away. The rest of the potato should be cooked immediately.

· Green potatoes, or potatoes where the eyes are sprouting, can be eaten; just cut away the eyes first. They are not rotten, but growing. Like other nightshades, sprouting potato shoots contain toxic bitter alkaloids. These compounds are denatured at high temperatures, so cooking greening potatoes is safe; just take care to thoroughly cook them to avoid stomachaches.

## COOKING

· Potatoes can be **baked, fried, roasted, boiled** into soup, or **steamed**.

· Potato peel is edible and is high in minerals, but some find it distasteful, especially if the potato is going bad, and prefer to remove the peels before cooking.

· **Baking:** When baking potatoes, it is usually best to cut them into chunks and use a generous amount of oil to ensure they cook evenly. Potatoes can be baked whole, but baking takes longer, and without oil, the skin toughens and the inside tends to be a bit dry.

· **Frying:** Add about a half inch (1 cm) of high-temperature oil to a frying pan and heat on high for a few minutes. Add chopped potatoes to the oil once it is hot—be careful not to let the oil splash. Flip the slices once the edges begin to brown. It may be necessary to reduce the stove heat to prevent burning. Well-fried potatoes will be crispy on the outside and soft on the inside.

- **Stir-frying:** It is possible to stir-fry potatoes with much less oil—but this is difficult because less oil means more stirring, and excessive stirring destroys the potato. Sometimes this effect is desirable. When stir-frying vegetables, try adding some potato and a little bit of water first. The potato will partially disintegrate and coat the veggies with a filling starch.

- **Steaming and boiling:** Steamed potato will be quite mushy and is often mashed completely after cooking. Boiled potato is rather bland and surprisingly dry. Boiled or steamed potato can be fried briefly in oil and flavorers to make it more savory, moist, and flavorful.

- **Cook time:** It takes longer to cook potato than you might expect. Potatoes can never get too mushy (they just become mashed potatoes), but undercooked hard potatoes don't taste very good and are difficult to digest. Make sure to cook potatoes thoroughly.

## SYNERGIES

- Potatoes can be roasted with other root vegetables like carrots and beets. They go great with other veggies like leafy greens or broccoli but must be cooked separately.

- Potatoes work well with all meat and mix quite well with beans.

- When making mashed potatoes, try sautéing onions first and mashing them in once they have browned. It's also nice to mash in well-cooked root vegetables like beets or carrots.

- Potatoes boiled into soup will partially disintegrate and add a starchy creaminess to the soup. This effect can be amplified with an immersion blender.

- Mixing milk or yogurt into mashed potatoes makes them creamier.

- Potatoes are quite bland and so require a lot of flavorers. Salt is a must. Potatoes absorb herbs quite well, especially rosemary. Some people like hot pepper. Give nutritional yeast a try!

### POTATO PANCAKES

Potato pancakes are a traditional eastern European dish. Here is how to make them:

- Grate potatoes and onions with a hand grater or food processor and then mix them together with eggs, flour, salt, and flavorers.

- Fill a pan with about a half inch (1 cm) of high-temperature oil and heat it for a few minutes.

- Use a large spoon to add a spoonful of the mixture to the hot oil and press down to make a sort of patty.

- Be very attentive while the pancakes are cooking—it is very easy to burn them. Flip them after they turn golden brown.

- When the pancakes are cooked, quickly remove them from the fryer and set them on a plate with a layer of paper towel to absorb the excess oil.

- The oil that remains in the pan at the end of cooking can be poured into a glass jar and saved to fry with again. It will have absorbed any spices you used.

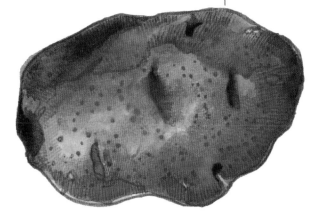

# Quinoa

Quinoa is a shrubby plant native to the Andes Mountains in Peru with highly nutritious seeds. It is one of the few carbohydrate sources with a complete set of all twenty-two essential amino acids.

## STORAGE

· Quinoa can be stored unrefrigerated in a dry place for several years.

## COOKING

· Try to rinse quinoa before boiling it. The seeds contain a protective coating to which some people have sensitivities.

· The best way to cook quinoa is to **boil** it.

· Cover quinoa with water deep enough to submerge your thumbnail and cook until the water is absorbed and the quinoa is soft. Add more water if necessary.

· Boil quinoa in vegetable stock for extra flavor.

## SYNERGIES

· Quinoa is very high in protein, so it goes great alongside meat or beans, and small portions can be quite filling.

· For extra crunch, try adding some nuts or bean sprouts.

· Try mixing some bell pepper or carrots into quinoa dishes for color.

· Sprouted quinoa can be mixed into bread dough to make it denser and heartier.

## SPROUTING

Sprouting grains is an excellent way to increase their nutritional content. As the seeds germinate and begin to grow, preservative chemicals break down and starch is converted into vitamins and easily absorbed mineral compounds. Here's how to sprout quinoa:

· Soak the quinoa in water for a few days, making sure to change the water about once every twelve hours.

· After a day or two, the already conspicuous root of the quinoa embryo will begin to grow and elongate.

· At this point, the living seeds are ready to be boiled and eaten. Sprouted quinoa cooks in just a couple of minutes.

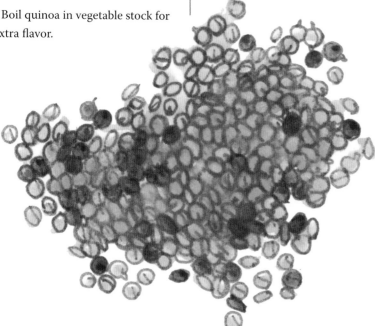

# Rice

Rice is a cereal grain native to southern China. The most well-known types of rice, white and brown, come not from genetics but a difference in processing. White rice has had the bran, a nutritious seed coat, removed. Brown rice retains the bran. Brown rice is more nutritionally complete than white rice, but it takes longer to cook.

## STORAGE

· Rice can be stored unrefrigerated in a dry place for several years.

## COOKING

· **Cook time:** The best way to cook rice is to **boil** it. Cook time varies between brown and white rice, with brown rice sometimes taking almost twice as long.

· Cover rice with water deep enough to submerge your thumbnail and cook until the water is absorbed and the rice is soft. Add more water if necessary.

· Boil rice in vegetable stock for extra flavor.

· Rice is usually a savory dish, but it can also be made into a delicious pudding similar to oatmeal. Try boiling rice with milk, dried fruit, nuts, sweeteners, cinnamon, and vanilla.

## SYNERGIES

· A good meal with rice should also have a large portion of vegetables. Try okra, cauliflower, or leafy greens. Beets are great because rice picks up their color quite well.

· Rice is extremely flexible and goes great with all sorts of protein. Meat, beans, tofu, and nuts are all great additions.

· Rice with cheese melted into it is an extremely simple and filling dish. Spinach or lettuce can add freshness.

### GENETICALLY MODIFIED RICE

· Golden rice tastes just like regular rice, but it looks yellow because it has been genetically modified to produce vitamin A.

· Golden rice was designed to address malnutrition (vitamin A deficiencies) in the developing world.

· While there is little documented risk in genetic modification, the socio-political injustice which often surrounds the development and distribution of GMOs should be cause for concern.

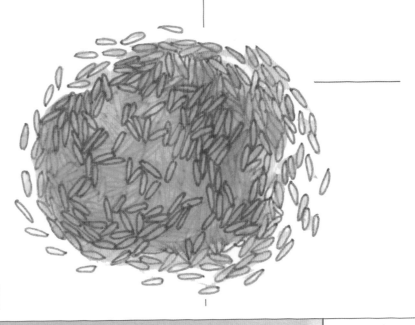

# Starchy Roots

Starchy roots (yam, taro, cassava, and kudzu) are a diverse group of plants used as a carbohydrate source, mostly in tropical regions sensitive to drought. They come from a variety of distantly related plant families, and many are not actually roots but tubers, corms, or rhizomes.

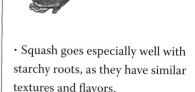

## STORAGE

· Starchy roots can be stored unrefrigerated for several weeks.

## COOKING

· Starchy roots can be **boiled**, **steamed**, **fried**, **roasted**, or **baked**.

· The skin of starchy roots is tough and should be peeled off before cooking.

· **Cook time:** Starchy roots can be quite dry and fibrous. They need to be cooked for a long time to soften the flavor.

· **Boiling:** Starchy roots should be peeled before boiling. After boiling, it's a good idea to add a lot of fat and flavorers.

· **Frying:** Cut the root into thin disks or strips that can easily be submerged in oil. Frying is complete when the root becomes soft.

· **Baking:** Starchy roots can be baked whole or cut into strips. When baking whole, the skin should be left on to preserve moisture. It is easy to remove with your fingers after cooking is complete. When baking cut pieces, be sure to use a generous amount of fat and water so that the root doesn't dry out.

## SYNERGIES

· Starchy roots can be very dry. To moisten them, try mashing them with milk or using yogurt as a condiment.

· Squash goes especially well with starchy roots, as they have similar textures and flavors.

· Starchy roots can be baked with large pieces of meat, where they will soak up the fluids that drip out.

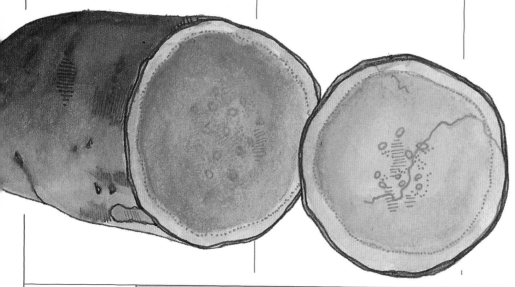

# Sweet Potato

Sweet potato is a viny plant with a starchy root native to Central America. Despite the similarity of name, sweet potato is only distantly related to common potato, which is a tuber, not a root.

### STORAGE

· Sweet potato can be stored unrefrigerated for several weeks.

· Moldy spots on a sweet potato can be cut away. Afterward, as long as the root is still hard, it can still be used. Soft sweet potatoes should be composted.

### COOKING

· Sweet potato can be **boiled**, **steamed**, **fried**, **roasted**, or **baked**.

· **Boiling:** Sweet potato goes great in soups, where it is sometimes boiled to the point where the flesh dissolves completely in the boiling water, producing a rich, sweet, and creamy broth.

· **Frying:** To fry sweet potato, peel it and cut it into thin disks or strips that can easily be submerged in oil. Frying is complete when the sweet potato becomes soft.

· **Stir-frying:** It is possible to stir-fry sweet potato, but the excessive stirring stir-frying requires tends to fragment the potato into a starchy mush that coats the rest of the vegetables in the stir-fry.

· **Baking:** In most cases, the sweet potato skin is removed before cooking because it is not very palatable. But when baking sweet potato whole, the skin should be left on to preserve moisture. When baking peeled pieces, be sure to use generous amounts of fats and flavorers.

Baking is done when the potato's orange color becomes brighter and more vibrant and the flesh softens.

### SYNERGIES

· Squash goes especially well with sweet potato, as they have similar textures and flavors. Sweet potato is very high in sugar, and so it goes well with either a sweet or savory palate.

· Mixing milk or yogurt into mashed sweet potatoes makes them creamier.

· Try baking sweet potato with apples or plantain to bring out the sweetness.

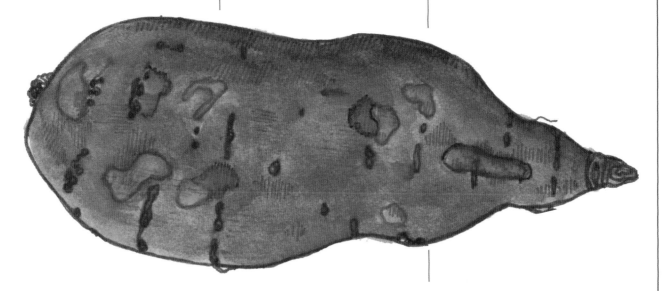

# protein

PROTEIN COMES FROM TWO SOURCES: plants and animals. The major plant sources of protein are nuts and beans, although whole grains and mushrooms provide a good amount of protein as well. Nuts are large seeds from hardwood trees, usually protected by a tough shell. Beans are the seeds from a family of plants called legumes, which are notable for their symbiotic relationship with nitrogen-fixing bacteria. Nitrogen is important because proteins are made up of chains of amino acids, which rely heavily on nitrogen for their structure. (The name *amino* comes from the nitrogen-bearing amine group -NH2.) The nitrogen-fixing bacteria in legumes ensure that bean plants have all the nitrogen they need to produce large, protein-packed seeds. While nuts and beans are relatively high in protein, they also have a lot of fiber, which means you need to eat much more of them by weight to obtain the same amount of protein that could be found in animal products. Additionally, animal protein sources contain all twenty-two kinds of amino acids needed to build the proteins that make up an animal body, as they came from living bodies themselves. In contrast, the plant proteins found in beans and nuts do not each provide all twenty-two amino acids when eaten on their own. Different plant proteins must be combined with one another to give the complete array of amino acids that your body needs. Getting the right mix of amino acids is so important that we actually have a taste receptor called umami that responds to amines specifically. The umami taste is what gives meat its rich and heavy flavor. Proteins are a vital and dense source of energy, so take special care to get enough protein, from a variety of sources.

# Bacon

Bacon is made by smoking, curing, and heavily salting thin strips of meat cut close to the skin from the sides and belly of a pig. Bacon is incredibly high in fat—it's actually a better fat source than protein source—so it should be eaten with moderation.

## STORAGE

· Bacon should be kept refrigerated and will keep for about two weeks.

· Rendered bacon fat can be stored unrefrigerated for several months.

## COOKING

· Bacon can be **baked, roasted, grilled,** or **fried.**

· **Frying:** To fry bacon, place strips in a frying pan and heat it on the stove. There is no need to add additional oil; the stovetop heat will melt the fat in the strips and the meat will fry in its own fat. Cooking takes about ten minutes—finished bacon will be shriveled, curled, and slightly crispy.

· **Baking:** To bake bacon, place strips on a baking pan and put it in the oven on a medium heat. Baking is an excellent method if you are trying to cook a large quantity of bacon that won't fit in a frying pan. Similar to frying, the oven heat will melt the bacon fat and the meat will fry in its own oil. Cooking takes about twenty minutes and the finished bacon will be shriveled, curved, and slightly crispy.

· **Rendering fat:** With either method, the melted bacon fat can be saved for later use. Simply pour the fat into a jar once the bacon has been removed from the pan. The fat can be used in place of butter or oil, but be mindful that it will make your food taste like bacon.

## SYNERGIES

· Bacon is very heavy and intense and is usually used to complement other foods rather than as a dish on its own. Bacon strips go great in sandwiches. Finely chopped bacon pieces add rich highlights to salads, stir-fries, and pasta dishes.

· Bacon and eggs are a traditional combination mostly because bacon fat is perfect for cooking eggs. It imbues them with a salty, smoky, meaty flavor.

· The heaviness of bacon can be balanced by a large portion of lettuce, spinach, or cooked leafy greens.

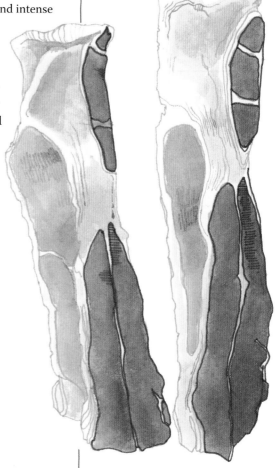

# Birds

The most common form of poultry is chicken. Chickens were domesticated about 5,000 years ago in Asia and are now the most populous birds on earth. Western cultures typically only eat the fleshy portions of birds, but in other societies, eating the feet and organs is quite common.

## STORAGE

· Poultry should be kept refrigerated and will keep for about a week.

· Bird meat can be frozen and will keep for about a year.

· Bad poultry is quite obvious. It will be discolored, slimy, and smell awful.

## COOKING

· Bird meat can be **baked, grilled, roasted, stir-fried**, or **boiled** into soup.

## BAKING

· To bake poultry, place it on a baking pan with a bit of water or oil. It is often nice to rub the meat with a mixture of spices or bake it on a bed of flavoring vegetables, root vegetables, or potatoes.

· Place the pan in the oven on a medium temperature. You may want to cover the pan with tinfoil or a large lid to keep in moisture.

· **Cook time:** Cook time will vary with food quantity but will likely take longer than an hour. When the meat is thoroughly cooked, you should be able to cut it with a knife and see a pale beige color without a hint of bloody pink or red.

## BOILING

· To make soup (or soup stock), completely cover the meat with water in a large pot.

· **Cook time:** Boil a whole bird for a couple hours or more. The longer the cook time, the more flavorful the broth.

· Toward the end of the boiling process, it is nice to add vegetables, flavorers, and maybe some potato or boiling grains. The meat can be removed and eaten separately or cut into the soup.

· It is good practice to make soup stock with the bird carcass that remains after eating the meat—there's lots of flavor and nutrition left in the skin and bones.

## STIR-FRYING

· Stir-frying bird meat is a nice method because it is by far the fastest.

· Cut the meat into small chunks and then heat it in a frying pan with a little bit of oil.

· Add some vegetables, flavorers, and maybe seeds or nuts for texture. Flavorful liquids, like citrus juice or coconut milk, add unique highlights and keep the meat from drying out.

· **Cook time:** The meat is thoroughly cooked when it changes to a light color without a hint of bloody red—usually in about twenty minutes.

# Hard Beans

Bean plants contain nitrogen-fixing bacteria which make bean protein rich and very desirable to predators. In defense, beans fill themselves with preservative compounds that are difficult to digest. Thus, beans need to be cooked extensively to make their protein available. A well-cooked stew of beans, vegetables, fat, and flavorers is the primary protein source of most cultures of the world.

## STORAGE

· Hard beans can be stored dry and unrefrigerated for several years.

· Presoaked beans can be kept refrigerated for over a week, but it is best to boil them right away.

## COOKING

· **Presoaking:** Hard beans should be presoaked for several hours before boiling. Soaking and boiling destroys preservative compounds that cause digestive issues. Beans have a reputation as gas producers because they are frequently undercooked and not presoaked.

· **Boiling:** Add plenty of water to a large soup pot and boil the beans until they are soft. Excess water can be strained away or used as broth for soup.

· **Cook time:** Most hard beans take over an hour, although soybeans take at least two hours.

· Once boiled, beans can subsequently be **baked**, **stir-fried**, or made into soup, chili, curry, stew, burgers, or hummus.

· Experiment with the flavor palate and amount of water added to make soup, chili, curry, or stew. These are different words and ethnic variations of the same basic mixture of vegetables, fats, flavorers, and sometimes dairy. Make sure to add the vegetables toward the end so they don't overcook.

· **Stir-frying and baking:** Boiled beans can be **stir-fried** or **baked** with fat, vegetables, and flavorers. This is a waterless version of the stew above.

## SYNERGIES

· Beans are quite bland and require a lot of added flavoring, especially salt. Their blandness makes them a wonderful canvas to experiment with spices. Endless flavorful and unique combinations are possible.

· Adding a bit of milk, plain yogurt, or cheese can balance out the flavor of too many strong spices.

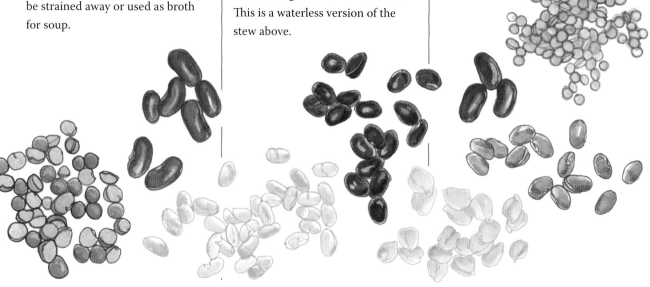

# Sproutable Beans

Sproutable beans are small and quick to germinate. They contain fewer preservative compounds and require shorter cook times than hard beans. They do not need to be presoaked before boiling. If they are soaked, the germination process begins, resulting in bean sprouts in a couple of days.

## STORAGE

· Sproutable beans remain edible for several years but will typically lose the ability to sprout after a year or two.

· Bean sprouts should be kept moist by changing their water every day. They need not be refrigerated and will keep for about a week.

## SPROUTING

· Sprouting beans is a great way to get the protein content of beans in a form that tastes fresh, green, and crunchy.

· Soak beans in water overnight.

· Dump out the extra water but keep the beans damp for the next few days.

· In a day or so, roots will start to emerge from the beans, and they are ready to eat.

## COOKING

· Sproutable beans can be boiled like hard beans. They do not need to be presoaked and take significantly less time to cook thoroughly than their larger brethren.

· Bean sprouts don't need to be cooked, as the sprouting process makes all the nutrients in the beans available for direct consumption.

· For hot dishes, add bean sprouts at the end of cooking. Cook them just long enough to heat them up, but not long enough to discolor them or make them mushy.

## SYNERGIES

· Bean sprouts and boiled beans go well in the same sorts of dishes, but they have a drastically different flavor and texture.

· Bean sprouts are crunchy and taste a bit like salad (they go well in salad, as it happens), whereas cooked beans are richer and earthier.

### HUMMUS

Hummus is a traditional Palestinian dish made with chickpeas, garlic, tahini, and oil. To make hummus:

· Blend boiled beans, oil, and whatever spices you like in a food processor to make a creamy paste.

· A standard flavor mixture is garlic, salt, and vinegar, but vinegar is not always necessary, and other flavors like hot peppers can be a nice addition. Adding a bit of water might be helpful to keep it from getting too oily.

· This is a fantastic way to reuse leftover beans, even if they are heavily spiced. Some of the best bean dips are made by accident by adding extra garlic and vinegar to an unusually spiced stew.

# Soybeans

Soybeans are the most protein-dense plant crop that is grown on an industrial scale. Soybeans are one of the few plant foods that are considered a complete protein, meaning that they contain all twenty-two essential amino acids. Their high protein content makes them correspondingly difficult to digest, and they must be boiled for significantly longer than other beans.

### STORAGE

· Soybeans can be stored dry and unrefrigerated for several years.

· Presoaked soybeans can be kept refrigerated for over a week, but it is best to boil them right away.

### COOKING

· Because soybeans are so difficult to digest, many processing methods have been developed. Tofu, tempeh, soy sauce, soybean oil, and soy milk are all made from processed soybeans. The easiest processing method is to make soy milk.

· **Boiling:** Soybeans must be boiled before anything else can be done with them. Soybeans need to boil for significantly longer than any other bean.

### MAKING SOY MILK

· Presoak soybeans.

· Toss them in a blender or food processor and make a purée.

· Boil the purée for several hours.

· Filter the purée from the soy milk with a cheesecloth after the mixture has cooled.

· Drink!

· Soy milk companies add things like sugar and carrageenan to make their soy milk sweeter and milkier. You can do the same if you want, but I prefer my soy milk to taste like soy.

### EDAMAME

· One way to get around the intense processing requirements of soybeans is to eat them while they are juvenile, before they become loaded with preservatives.

· Immature green soybeans, known as edamame, are eaten fresh in their pods.

· Edamame can be **boiled**, **steamed**, or **stir-fried** in about ten minutes.

### SYNERGIES

· Edamame can be mixed into rice to make the dish more filling, but not overly heavy.

· Try making a soybean curry with ginger, coconut milk, and turmeric.

· It's nice to sprinkle a few soybeans and some salt over rice. Properly cooked soybeans tend to be less mealy and more meaty and chewy than other bean varieties.

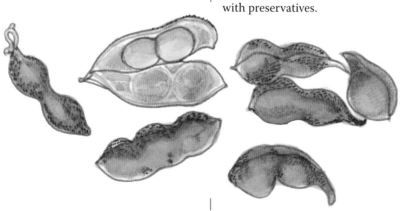

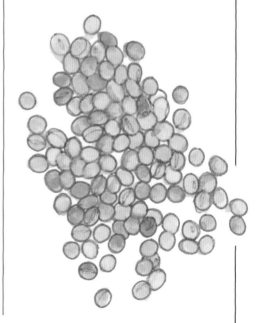

# Eggs

Eggs are reproductive cells surrounded by hard shells produced in the ovaries of all birds. Eggs are one of the most nutritionally complete foods you can eat because they contain all the material necessary to create a growing chick.

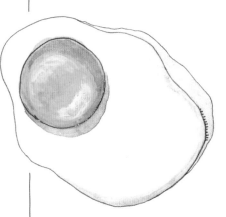

### STORAGE

· Eggs can be kept unrefrigerated for a couple of weeks or refrigerated for over a month.

· You can tell a bad egg by its smell. Any egg that doesn't reek of sulfur is safe to eat as long as it's cooked fully.

· Don't eat eggs that have been sitting in the carton cracked.

### COOKING

· Eggs can be **boiled**, **fried**, **stir-fried**, or **baked**.

· **Cook time:** Eggs cook quite quickly when exposed to heat. Eggs are done when all of the liquid has solidified.

· **Boiling:** Eggs can be boiled whole or poached by cracking them into boiling water. To make peeling easier, immediately soak hard-boiled eggs in cold water. This causes the outer layers of the shell to separate from the cooked flesh.

· **Frying:** To fry eggs, crack them into a pan with a little bit of fat. Eggs can be fried intact or scrambled to mix the yolk with the white. Sometimes it is nice to scramble the eggs in a bowl beforehand so that cheese, milk, vegetables, or flavorers can be mixed in.

· **Baking:** To make quiche (or something similar), mix a large number of eggs with dairy, vegetables, and flavorers together in a shallow pan and bake for an hour at a low temperature. The baked eggs bind everything together.

· **Stir-frying:** Eggs can be used as a binder and thickener for stir-fries and soups. Eggs make things stick together and taste heartier.

### SYNERGIES

· Milk and cheese make the eggs heartier and fluffier.

· Eggs also work surprisingly well with nutmeg, which brings out unexpected flavors.

· Eggs can be scrambled with most delicate vegetables. Mushrooms, tomatoes, and spinach work particularly well.

· Try frying an egg or two with a generous amount of rice and vegetables. The eggs will nicely bind the rice and veggies together.

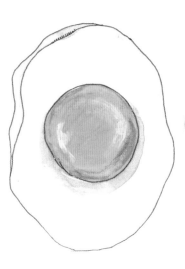

# Fish

Wild fish has been a major source of protein in the human diet for millennia. As the human population grows, wild fish populations shrink. Today we rely quite heavily on aquaculture; more than half the fish we eat comes from fish farms.

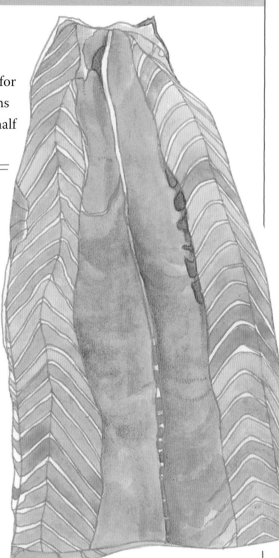

## STORAGE

· Fresh fish is extremely perishable. Even when refrigerated, it only lasts a few days.

· Fish can be kept frozen for several months.

· Bad fish will be discolored and smell awful.

## COOKING

· Fish can be **baked**, **fried**, **grilled**, **roasted**, or **boiled** into soup.

· **Baking:** The simplest method of fish cooking is baking. To bake fish, place it on a pan and put it in the oven on high heat.

· **Frying:** To fry fish, place it on a frying pan and cook with high heat. The fish may need to be flipped once, especially if you are cooking without a lid. Avoid stirring the fish in the pan, as the delicate flesh will flake apart.

· **Boiling:** To make fish soup, cover the meat with water in a large pot and boil for half an hour or more. Add fresh vegetables and flavorers at the end of the boiling process.

· **Cook time:** Cook times for all methods are similar and will vary with fish weight. Cooking usually takes under half an hour. The fish is done when its color pales and switches from slightly transparent to completely opaque. Undercooked fish is sometimes preferable but should only be eaten if the fish is extremely fresh and from a close local source.

· **Stir-frying:** Leftover cooked fish is an excellent addition to a stir-fry. Cut it up into small pieces and mix it in with fresh vegetables and boiled grains. The fish will flake apart and add a rich, fishy tone to your meal.

## SYNERGIES

· Classic fish flavorers include parsley, dill, and sour citrus, but don't be limited to a tangy palate.

· Fresh fish should be served with some sort of carbohydrate, usually boiled grains or pasta. Leftover fish can be flaked apart and used as a sort of bread spread, similar to canned tuna, but much tastier.

· Fish takes less time to cook than other meat. Fish goes well with fresh green vegetables with similarly short cook times.

# Mammals

Cows, pigs, sheep, and goats were all domesticated about 10,000 years ago in the Middle East. These livestock animals became a reliable source of protein, fabric, and dairy. Most importantly, they provided the muscle power to plow large fields, as well as an efficient way to transform unwanted plant waste into fertilizer and protein.

### STORAGE

· Red meat should be kept refrigerated and will keep for about a week.

· Red meat can be frozen and will keep for about a year.

· Bad meat is clearly bad. It will be discolored and slimy and smell awful.

### COOKING

· Red meat can be **baked, stir-fried, grilled, roasted**, or **boiled** into soup.

#### BAKING

· To bake red meat, place it on a baking pan with a bit of water or oil.

· It is often nice to rub the meat with a mixture of spices or bake it on a bed of flavoring vegetables, root vegetables, or potatoes.

· Place the pan in the oven on a medium temperature. You may want to cover the pan with tinfoil or a large lid to keep in moisture.

· **Cook time:** Cook time will vary with quantity but will likely take longer than an hour. When the meat is thoroughly cooked, you should be able to cut it with a knife and see a dark brown color without a hint of bloody red.

#### BOILING

· To make soup (or soup stock), completely cover the meat with water in a large pot and boil it for a couple of hours or more.

· **Cook time:** The longer the cook time, the more flavorful the broth. It is not possible to overboil meat for soup.

· Toward the end of the boiling process, it is nice to add vegetables, flavorers, and maybe some potato or boiling grains. The meat can be removed and eaten separately or cut into the soup.

· It is nice to boil soup with fattier cuts of meat with lots of bone, like brisket or spare rib. Large leftover bones also make an excellent soup stock when boiled for several hours.

### STIR-FRYING

· Stir-frying is a nice method because it is by far the fastest—no more than twenty minutes.

· Cut the meat into small chunks or thick slices and then heat it in a frying pan with a little bit of oil. Add some vegetables, flavorers, and maybe seeds or nuts for texture.

### SYNERGIES

· Red meat goes well with most vegetables. It can be stir-fried with the delicate green ones and baked or boiled with heartier root vegetables.

· Red meat can be improved with a certain amount of tart sweetness. Try cooking it with apples, tomatoes, citrus, or onions.

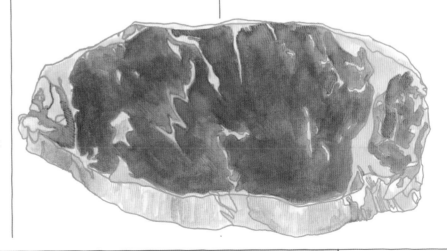

# Nuts

Nuts are the large, shelled seeds of hardwood trees and are high in fat and protein. Peanuts are not actually nuts—they are a kind of bean—but are cooked with like nuts because of their similar flavor and texture.

## STORAGE

· Nuts can be stored unrefrigerated for several months.

· Rancid nuts will taste sour and chalky.

## COOKING

· Nuts can be eaten **raw** but are great **stir-fried, roasted,** and **baked**. They can also be **ground** into nut butter.

· **Soaking:** Raw nuts contain preservative compounds that make them difficult to digest. Soak raw nuts in water for a few hours to break down these compounds.

· Nuts are an incredibly useful garnish because they add crunch.

· **Cook time:** Nuts don't have a set cook time and can be cooked for any period of time without ill effect.

## NUT BUTTER

Nut butter is high in fat and protein. It's great when you are in a rush. It makes an excellent sauce on stir-fries and is a staple bread spread.

· **Grinding:** To make nut butter, leave nuts in a food processor for over ten minutes. The nuts will break apart, and after a few minutes, the nut oils will seep out and bind the mixture together with a creamy texture. Leave the food processor running until your desired consistency is reached.

## NUT MILK

Nut milks have recently become popular as a high-protein alternative to cow's milk or soy milk. It is easy to make, but it consumes a huge quantity of nuts. Here's how to make almond milk:

· **Soak:** Soak nuts overnight or even longer. The longer you soak them, the creamier your milk will be.

· **Blend:** Pour out the soaking water and replace with fresh water. Purée this mixture in a powerful blender for several minutes. Experiment with water quantity; the less water you use, the thicker your milk will be, but the less of it you'll have.

· **Strain:** After the nuts are thoroughly blended, strain the nut pulp from the milk with cheesecloth. The pulp can be baked into bread or used to add texture to stir fries.

· Drink!

## SYNERGIES

· Nuts work well in desserts or savory dishes. Their flavor is rich but mild and blends well with most palates.

· Nuts can be eaten alone or mixed into most dishes to add a nice texture. They go great in salads. Add them to dishes whole or toss them in a food processor for a few seconds if you want the crunch to be smaller.

· Nuts work particularly well with tofu. Try stir-frying a mixture of tofu, rice, nuts, and leafy greens, flavored with ginger and turmeric.

# Tempeh

Tempeh is made from soybeans that have been fermented and caked together by a fungus. The fermentation process, developed in Indonesia, partially breaks the soybeans down, making tempeh easier to digest and higher in vitamins than other soy products.

## STORAGE

· Tempeh should be kept refrigerated and will keep for several weeks.

· Tempeh can be frozen and will keep for several months.

· Because tempeh is fermented, it rarely rots. However, it can dry out and become unpalatable if it's left exposed to open air.

## COOKING

· Tempeh can be **baked, roasted, grilled, stir-fried,** or **steamed**.

· **Cook time:** Tempeh can be eaten after minimal cooking, but it softens with longer cook times. Eat tempeh when it softens to your liking.

· **Baking:** To bake tempeh, place it on a pan with oil, water, and plenty of flavorers. Put it in the oven on low heat. It is easy to dry tempeh out, so check it often. Baking should take no longer than half an hour.

· **Stir-frying:** To stir-fry tempeh, cut it into pieces and heat it in a frying pan with oil, water, spices, and vegetables. Stir-frying takes about fifteen minutes.

· **Steaming:** Steaming is nice because it is quick, but it tends to leave the tempeh flavorless. Make sure to add lots of flavorers at the end.

## SYNERGIES

· Mushrooms go especially well with tempeh since the fermentation process already leaves the soybeans with a mushroomy taste.

· Tempeh is rather bland on its own and should be cooked with plenty of flavorers.

· Use tempeh as you would an animal protein. It should be served with generous helpings of both vegetables and carbohydrates.

· Try adding nuts to tempeh dishes. The nuts add texture and complement the tempeh's already nutty flavor.

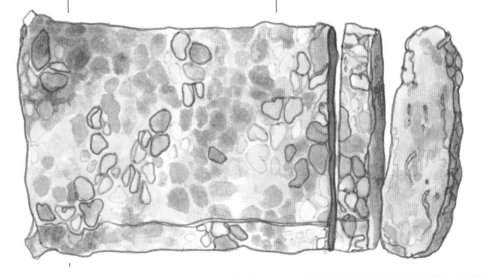

# Tofu

Tofu is made by using acid to coagulate the proteins found in soy milk into a dense brick. Tofu contains much of the nutrients contained in whole soybeans but with less of the fiber and preservative compounds that make soy difficult to digest.

## STORAGE

· Tofu should be kept refrigerated and will keep for over a month.

· Tofu can be frozen for over a year, but the freezing process makes tofu very rubbery and only suitable for soups.

· Rancid tofu will be yellow, sour, and slimy.

## COOKING

· Tofu can be eaten **raw**, **baked**, **fried**, **stir-fried**, **grilled**, **roasted**, **steamed**, or **boiled**.

· Tofu comes in many densities, from soft to firm, each with different cooking properties. I prefer to cook with extra-firm tofu.

· **Cook time:** Tofu comes pre-processed and requires very little cooking.

· **Raw:** Tofu comes precooked, so cooking it further is optional. Tofu is most frequently cooked because cooking adds flavor to what would otherwise be a very bland food, but raw tofu can be flavored too.

· It is nice to marinate raw tofu slices with soy sauce, oil, and seeds for texture and eat it with salad.

· **Stir-frying:** Tofu becomes denser and more flavorful with longer cooktimes. It is best to stir tofu in the pan as little as possible so it doesn't break up.

· Sometimes fragmented tofu is desirable. Heavy stirring can make a tofu scramble with a similar texture and flavor to scrambled eggs.

· **Frying:** Heat a pan with about half an inch (1 cm) of high-temperature oil. Put the tofu in after the oil is hot. The tofu is done when the outsides become crispy and yellow brown, usually in about twenty minutes.

· It is nice to add whole spice seeds while frying the oil, like pepper, cardamom, or mustard.

· **Baking:** Baking is a great method for tofu because the baking process removes much of the water in tofu, giving it a better texture.

· Bake tofu with lots of flavorers and vegetables. Don't skimp on the oil or salt.

## SYNERGIES

· Tofu can be baked with hearty vegetables like carrots or kohlrabi or stir-fried with leafy greens.

· Nuts or seeds are key to most tofu dishes. They add a necessary crunch.

· Tofu should be served along with some sort of carbohydrate, be it boiled grains or pasta, potatoes, or bread.

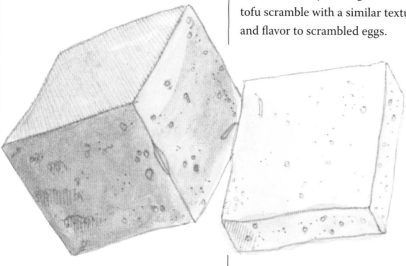

# Shellfish

Crustaceans (lobsters, crabs, and shrimp) are a group of animals closely related to insects with hard outer shells that contain succulent white meat. Shellfish are scavengers; they dwell on the bottom of the sea eating scraps that have fallen from above.

## STORAGE

· Crustaceans are extremely perishable and are frequently purchased live to ensure freshness.

· Don't cook shellfish that has been sitting for more than a few days.

· Crustaceans freeze quite well and can be kept frozen for several months.

## COOKING

· Shellfish can be a wonderful addition to all sorts of dishes, but is almost always **boiled** before further preparation.

## BOILING

· Boiling live shellfish can be ethically dubious for some, depending on your views about pain and consciousness. Some people prefer to stab lobsters behind the eyes before cooking them, but whether this minimizes pain is anyone's guess.

· It's best to add shellfish to already-boiling water so the meat cooks as quickly as possible.

· Crustaceans come from a marine environment, so it's important to heavily salt the water they are boiled in so the meat doesn't lose its natural salt.

· Shellfish is done when its shell becomes brightly colored (lobsters and most crabs turn red) and the flesh becomes firm and white.

## SYNERGIES

· Shellfish often goes well with a sour palate. Try boiling shrimp in a sauce made from tomato, sour citrus, cilantro, and dill.

· Unlike other meats, crustaceans are not very fatty, so it's usually a good idea to cook them with butter or oil.

· Boiling lobster with beets makes the flesh turn pink.

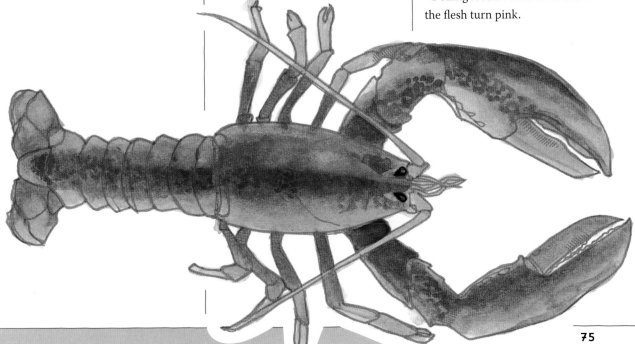

# fruits

FRUIT (ALONG WITH DAIRY) is special as an ingredient type because it was evolutionarily designed to be eaten by you. The botanical definition of a fruit is the portion of a plant that ripens and contains seeds. Plants make most fruit with the explicit hope that an animal will come along and eat the fruit, swallow its seeds, and then excrete them somewhere new, along with a nice dose of fertilizer. Because natural selection has been adapting fruit for millions of years to be enticing for animals to eat, very little needs to be done to prepare it for consumption. It is rarely cooked. In fact, the fruits that do need to be cooked, like squash and eggplant, are colloquially considered vegetables because intuition dictates that fruit is not a food that is cooked. However, fruit does spoil very easily, so many preservative measures have been developed to make fruit last longer. Juicing is a popular option, as is drying. Fruit compote (like apple sauce) requires less fancy equipment. Fruit is a remarkably complete food source. It has evolved to be packed with sugar, vitamins, and minerals. Because fruit is so well rounded nutritionally, it makes a great snack when you're in a rush. It's almost a complete meal in itself.

# Apples

Apples come from a flowering tree in the rose family native to Kazakhstan. Apples are one of the few fruit trees that do better in cold climates than warm ones. Apples have been central to Western diets and mythologies for millennia.

## STORAGE

· Most commercially available apples are harvested just before ripening and then stored in refrigerated and sealed buildings until the time comes for market, sometimes months later. At that point the apples are sprayed with ethylene gas to induce ripeness and shipped to market.

· Apples can be kept unrefrigerated for about two weeks, but refrigeration will allow them to last longer.

## COOKING

· Apples are most commonly eaten **raw**, but they can also be **baked**, **stir-fried, boiled** into applesauce, or **juiced**.

· Apples vary greatly in quality. As apples age they grow mealy, and some cultivars simply don't grow as well as others. But an apple of any quality, even highly bruised or partially rotten, will always make excellent juice.

· Aging or mealy apples can still be used in bakes and stir-fries, and they make great applesauce.

· Apples retain their texture after cooking much better than most other fruits.

· Bake apples with meat or add apples to a meat stir-fry to add a subtle sweetness and slight crunch.

· Squeeze a bit of sour citrus on apple slices to prevent them from oxidizing in the air and turning brown.

## SYNERGIES

· A quick, filling, and crunchy snack can be made from apples, cheese, nut butter, and raw carrots.

· Apples and onions have similar sugar content and go surprisingly well together.

· Cooked apples can add sweetness to plantain, oats, or sweet potato. Try flavoring them with ginger.

### APPLESAUCE

Applesauce is a great way to make use of apples that are going bad. Here's how to make it:

· Cut the fruit into chunks. Remove the seeds and stems.

· Put the chunks in a pot and heat for about an hour.

· Stir the cooked fruit together. It may be helpful to use an immersion blender to get the consistency right.

· It's nice to add sweet spices like cinnamon or cloves or a bit of lemon juice.

· Fresh warm applesauce is a wonderful thing. It can be eaten alone or mixed into yogurt or oatmeal.

# Avocado

Avocado comes from a flowering tree native to central Mexico. Its fruit has a uniquely high fat content, which makes the flesh rich and creamy rather that sweet and tart like most other fruits.

## STORAGE

· Avocado is usually sold hard and unripe. The fruit should be left out and not eaten until it feels slightly soft.

· To speed ripening, place avocados in a sealed container to capture the ethylene gas they emit. Adding a banana to the mixture will also speed ripening because bananas excrete a large amount of ethylene.

· Avocado can usually be stored unrefrigerated for about a week, depending on ripeness when purchased.

· If an avocado feels overly mushy, but you are not ready to eat it, put it in the fridge. Refrigeration slows the ripening process slightly.

## COOKING

· Avocado should be eaten **raw** and should never be cooked.

· Avocado can be cut into slices and eaten on its own or in salad, used as a bread spread, or mashed into guacamole.

## SYNERGIES

· Avocado is very chemically similar to cheese, and they go quite well together.

· Avocado goes great with any raw plant like carrot, radish, lettuce, spinach, celery, or tomato.

· Avocado and nuts make a great creamy-crunchy combo.

· Avocado makes an excellent bread spread on its own.

### GUACAMOLE

Guacamole is a superb dip or bread spread, and is a great way to make the most out of avocados that may be too mushy to eat. Here's how to make it:

· Scoop several avocados into a large bowl.

· Add lime or lemon juice, diced tomatoes, salt, and finely chopped onions or garlic.

· You can experiment with various flavorers, but the sour citrus juice is essential to prevent excess oxidation.

· Mash all the ingredients together with a large spoon.

· Serve with bread or chips!

# Bananas

Bananas are a seedless, sterile hybrid fruit of two different species of broad-leaved, tropical plants native to Southeast Asia. There is no dramatic genetic distinction between bananas and plantains, which are also hybrids of the same two species. Bananas are softer and sweeter and can be eaten raw.

## STORAGE

· Bananas are harvested when green so they can be shipped more easily. They are then sprayed with ethylene gas, a hormone produced by ripening fruit that induces further fruit ripening. They will continue to ripen after purchase.

· Bananas also emit a lot of ethylene gas, so they can be placed in a sealed container with unripe fruits to induce them to ripen.

· A banana that is slightly green when purchased will ripen in a few days. Bananas are best eaten when they are yellow and just slightly soft. Softer with little brown spots is okay if you like your bananas sweet and mushy. When the spots enlarge and become black, the banana is usually too soft to eat alone but can still be used as a fruity sweetening mush in many dishes.

· Overripe bananas can be frozen to preserve them. If possible, peel the banana and place it in a container before freezing. If the banana is too mushy for this, it can be frozen whole, but it will be difficult to peel later.

· Never put whole bananas in the fridge. Refrigeration destroys the peel.

## COOKING

· Bananas are usually eaten **raw** but can also be **blended** into pudding, **baked** into bread or pie, or **frozen** for ice cream or smoothies.

· To blend bananas into pudding, simply peel a bunch and blend them in a bowl by hand or with an immersion blender. It is sometimes nice to add flavorers like vanilla or cinnamon.

· Banana pudding is easily frozen into banana ice cream; just toss it in the freezer. If possible, try to take the freezing pudding out of the freezer a few times during the freezing process and give it a good mix with an immersion blender so that the ice crystals don't get too large and the whole thing doesn't turn into a brick.

· Use chunks of frozen whole bananas for smoothies or as ice cubes in fruity drinks.

## SYNERGIES

· Ripe or overripe banana makes an excellent bread spread. Partially mash it and spread it with a fork.

· Try a snack of banana, yogurt, nuts, and cinnamon.

· A banana with nut butter spread on top can be surprisingly filling.

· Bananas are fantastic at giving fruit smoothies a creamy texture if you don't want to use dairy.

# Berries

Berries are small, delicate fruits that come from a diverse array of plant species. Berries are notably fragile. Their skins are quite thin, which makes them difficult to ship and store and thus very expensive. However, berries are some of the most common edible wild plants. Even in urban areas, it's not uncommon to find a blackberry bush or mulberry tree hidden on an overlooked street corner.

## STORAGE

· Berries spoil extremely easily and should always be refrigerated. They last a few days at best.

· Berries are very easily frozen and can be kept for about a year.

## COOKING

· Berries are best eaten **raw** but can be **frozen**, **baked** into pastries, or **boiled** into jam or compote.

· Of all fruit, berries are perhaps best suited to freezing because of their small size. Frozen berries make a nice cold treat on their own. They make great ice cubes in fruity drinks and won't dilute the drink as they melt. They also go great in smoothies and work just as well in baked goods as fresh berries.

· Purée berries in a blender and then pour the mix into ice cube trays or ice-pop molds to make fresh ice pops.

### JELLY AND JAM

Here's how to make jam or jelly:

· Cut the fruit into chunks. Remove any pits, stems, or inedible peel.

· Put the chunks in a pot and add a whole lot of sugar and pectin if you've got it. The sugar acts as a gelling agent and makes the jam smooth and shiny.

· Heat the mixture for about half an hour. The longer you cook it, the more water will boil off and the thicker the product will be.

· Stir the cooked fruit together. It may be helpful to use an immersion blender to get the consistency right.

## SYNERGIES

· Berries go great with nuts, oatmeal, and yogurt.

· Frozen berries are wonderful in smoothies. Simple is usually better. It's surprising how tasty frozen berries and bananas can be when blended with water.

· Berries are an asset in any fruit salad.

# Citrus

Citrus are a genus of small evergreen fruit trees native to Southeast Asia. Citrus are notable for their tough, colorful rinds that protect slices of particularly juicy fruit within. The juice ranges from sweet to quite sour and is high in citric acid; hence the name *citrus*.

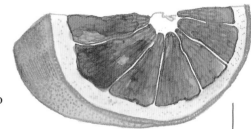

## STORAGE

· Citrus will keep for a couple of weeks unrefrigerated and a bit longer if refrigerated.

## COOKING

· Citrus are mostly eaten **raw**, but they are frequently **juiced** and can be **cooked** into marmalade.

· Citrus are particularly easy to juice and can be juiced effectively by hand (although a juicing appliance is much more efficient). Simply cut them in half and squeeze.

· Citrus juice makes an excellent flavorer for all sorts of dishes, particularly stir-fried meat or boiled grains.

· To make marmalade, just heat peeled citrus on the stove for a while. Add sweeteners as desired.

## SYNERGIES

· It's often nice to squeeze some citrus juice into boiling grains. The juice adds a sweet tanginess.

· Try using citrus juice when stir-frying meat or tofu.

· Citrus can add a nice highlight to traditional vegetable salads, especially salads that use a lot of sweet tomatoes.

· If you don't have the quantity or time to make fresh squeezed orange or grapefruit juice, it's usually all right to juice just a few and then dilute substantially with water. The drink will still taste quite fruity.

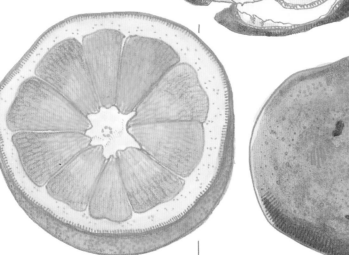

# Sour Citrus

Citrus hybridize quite easily and come in many sizes and colors. The particular color of a citrus fruit is not an indicator of ripeness but actually an indicator of wintering. Citrus grown at the equator remain green when ripe. Only when a citrus has experienced a cool period does its flesh become a color other than green.

## STORAGE

· Sour citrus will keep for a couple of weeks unrefrigerated and a bit longer if refrigerated.

## COOKING

· Sour citrus are not typically eaten on their own, but their juice is used as a garnish in many dishes. Think of sour citrus more like a spice than a fruit.

· Grated sour citrus peel (zest) can also be used to add flavor to baked goods.

## SYNERGIES

· Try stewing or stir-frying meat with coconut milk and sour citrus.

· Sour citrus juice can be used as a replacement for vinegar in many cases. It goes great in salad dressing.

· Sprinkle sour citrus over cut fruit to prevent it from oxidizing and turning brown.

### LEMONADE

· The trick to good lemonade is getting the balance right between the three ingredients: sour citrus juice, sugar, and water.

· How sweet, sour, or watery the lemonade is is a matter of personal taste. It is usually best to add the lemon juice to the water first to get the strength right and then add a small amount of sugar. Much less sugar is needed than most people expect.

· Limes, grapefruit, or even oranges can be really nice additions. Milder citrus evens out the flavor of the lemonade while making it more subtle and complex.

# Coconut

Coconuts are the very large and multilayered seeds of the coconut palm, a large, tree-like plant native to the tropical Pacific. Coconuts are designed to float on ocean water for many months before reaching a new beach and germinating. Their thick husk and hard shell prevent salt water from damaging the seed, and the huge fatty interior ensures the seedling has the best start possible in poor, sandy soils.

## FORMS

### YOUNG COCONUT

Young coconut has a green outer husk and a watery interior. The water inside is full of sugar and minerals. It is incredibly nutritious and has been used for blood transfusions in tropical battle zones. In younger coconuts, the sides of the seed wall are lined with a thick white jelly that is quite delicious when eaten fresh.

### MATURE COCONUT

As the coconut ages, the outer shell browns, the interior water is absorbed, and the coconut jelly solidifies into a hard, fatty cake called copra. Copra can be eaten as is, but it is frequently processed into oil or grated to make coconut flakes for confections.

### COCONUT MILK

Coconut milk is made by passing the hardening copra jelly through a cheesecloth before it is completely solidified.

### COCONUT WATER

Coconut water is derived directly from the interior of young coconuts.

## STORAGE

· Young coconut need not be refrigerated but should be eaten in about a week or so to keep the water from fermenting.

· Mature copra, whether in chunks, flakes, or canned as milk, need not be refrigerated and will last for many months.

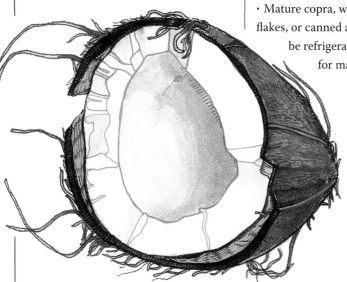

## COOKING

· Most coconut products are eaten **raw**, with the exception of coconut milk.

· Coconut water is surprisingly filling and is packed with minerals commonly known as electrolytes.

· Coconut milk is an excellent thickener for soups. It can be used to add weight to stir-fries and works especially well with meat. It is a staple in many bean curries and can be used to flavor boiled grains.

· Coconut flakes have a tendency to be quite dry. Make sure whatever you add them to has plenty of moisture to accommodate.

## SYNERGIES

· Try boiling grains in a mixture of coconut milk and water. The coconut milk adds a delightful, rich creaminess without as much weight as dairy.

· Add coconut milk to an especially spicy curry to balance out the flavor.

· Yogurt can be flavored with coconut milk, vanilla, and cinnamon. The two kinds of creaminess complement each other quite well.

# Cucumber

Cucumbers are large, ground-dwelling plants with broad leaves native to India. They are members of the squash family and are closely related to melons and pumpkin.

## STORAGE

· Cucumbers should be refrigerated and will keep for about two weeks.

· The flesh of a cucumber should be opaque greenish white. When the flesh starts to become clear, cells are dying and water is leaking out. Clear flesh is not very tasty.

## COOKING

· Cucumber is most often eaten **raw**. Heat is rarely added, but other processing methods are common, like **blending, pickling,** or **juicing**.

· Cucumbers are often peeled, but this is not necessary. The peel is edible and full of minerals.

· **Blending:** Put cucumbers in a food processor with flavorers to make a cool dipping sauce or gazpacho.

· **Pickling:** Soak cucumbers in salt, vinegar, and other flavorers for an hour to a few days to make crunchy pickles.

## SYNERGIES

· Cucumbers go great in salads with raw vegetables like bell peppers, carrots, celery, lettuce, radish, or spinach.

· Try serving a cold bulgur wheat salad with cucumber, avocado, olives, and tomatoes.

· Experiment with some unique flavors in a cucumber salad— maybe add horseradish or nutritional yeast?

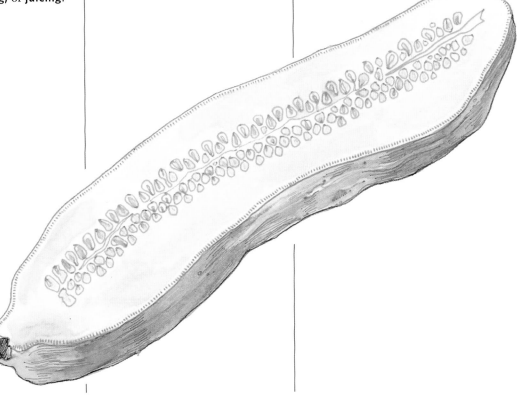

# Dried Fruits

Drying fruit was one of the earliest forms of food preservation. Dried fruits contain almost the same nutritional content as fresh fruit but will last for many months. Traditionally, fruit was dried in the sun, but today most fruit is dried in dehydrators, which are basically low-temperature ovens.

### STORAGE

· Dried fruit can be stored unrefrigerated for several months.

### COOKING

· Dried fruit is mostly eaten **raw** and makes an excellent snack in a hurry but can also be **baked** or **boiled**.

· **Baking:** Dried fruit can be baked into bread, cookies, or granola. When baking dried fruit, make sure there is enough moisture in the rest of the dish that the fruit does not dry out further and burn.

· **Boiling:** Boiling dried fruit partially reconstitutes it and will make it plump and juicy. It adds a nice texture and flavor to boiled dishes like oatmeal, applesauce, or fruit compote.

· Dried fruit can be used as a sweetener in addition to or as a replacement for sugar. The sweetness it adds is more complex, tart, and less intense than traditional sweeteners. Dates are especially good at adding sweetness.

### DRYING FRUIT

You can dry fruit on your own, although it can be quite labor intensive. The general principle is to heat the fruit with a low heat for a long time. The low heat sucks the water out of the fruit without cooking it much. Commercial dehydrators are built to maximize surface area, but drying can be done (tediously) in a kitchen oven.

#### TO DRY FRUIT

· Cut the fruit into thin slices and lay them on a pan.

· Put the pan in the oven on a low temperature.

· Check the fruit every twenty minutes or so to make sure it's not burning. You may need to flip the slices at some point.

### SYNERGIES

· Dried fruit goes great in cereal and yogurt or sprinkled on top of salads.

· Dried fruit and oats are natural friends. Dried fruit is central to a tasty serving of oatmeal or granola.

· Dried fruit and nuts make a very filling and highly portable snack that will stay tasty even if left in a bag for weeks.

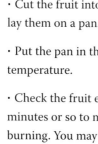

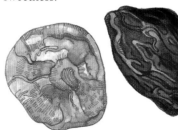

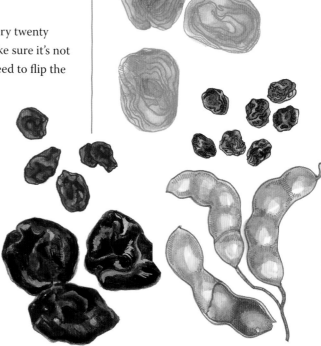

# Grapes

Grapes are the fruit of a viny plant native to the northern Middle East. Yeast grows naturally on grape skins, making fermentation quite easy. This partially explains the prevalence of wine in so many ancient cultures and religions.

## STORAGE

· Grapes should be kept refrigerated and will keep for about a week.

· Grapes can be frozen and will keep for several months.

## COOKING

· Grapes are best eaten **raw**, but they are also quite nice when **frozen**.

· Frozen grapes make a delicious cold snack. They also go great in smoothies and can be used as ice cubes in fruity drinks.

· Oddly enough, grapes don't juice very well in home-scale appliance juicers.

· To make jam, just heat grapes in a pan for a while. Add sugar as desired.

## SYNERGIES

· Grapes go well with just about all other fruit.

· Grapes can be nice in a green salad, along with nuts and cheese.

### FERMENTING WINE

Grape juice (or any other fruit juice) can be very easily fermented into wine or hard cider. All you need is a sealable bottle, some yeast, a balloon, and some patience. Here's how:

· Pour the juice into the bottle and add a sprinkle of yeast. Stretch the balloon over the mouth of the bottle.

· The yeast will begin to convert the sugar in the juice into alcohol and carbon dioxide. The balloon will expand with excess $CO_2$ and keep other contaminants from getting inside.

· After a few weeks, pour the liquid through a strainer to filter out the solids and then return it to the bottle and seal it with the cap. Fermentation will continue, and your drink will naturally carbonate itself.

· Keep the drink refrigerated and drink it within a few weeks. Make sure to open it periodically to let the excess $CO_2$ escape.

# Kiwi

Kiwi is the fruit of a viny plant native to southern China. The modern kiwi was cultivated in New Zealand about 100 years ago. The kiwi name was introduced as a marketing strategy aimed to highlight the geographic origin of the cultivar by comparing it to the national bird of New Zealand. Prior to New Zealand cultivation, kiwis were called Chinese gooseberry.

## STORAGE

· Kiwis should be kept refrigerated and will keep for about a week. Ripe kiwis should be slightly soft.

· Unripe kiwis will ripen faster if exposed to ethylene gas. To ripen them quickly, put them in a container with a banana.

## COOKING

· Kiwis are best eaten **raw**, but they can also be **cooked** into fruit compote.

· Kiwi peel is completely edible and does not need to be cut from the fruit before eating.

· Kiwi flesh contains high quantities of a protein-dissolving enzyme. Avoid mixing fresh kiwi with dairy, as it will curdle milk. Cooked kiwi can be added to dairy without a problem.

· To make kiwi compote, peel it and heat it on the stove for about an hour.

## SYNERGIES

· A kiwi can be eaten on its own like an apple or cut in half and scooped out with a spoon.

· Try chopping kiwi into a fruit salad with some nuts.

### FRUIT SMOOTHIE

Fruit smoothies can be made with frozen fruit or fruit that is about to go bad. Kiwis always make a nice addition. Making a fruit smoothie is exceptionally easy.

· Cut fruit into large chunks and mix it in a blender.

· Experiment with consistency—bananas add creaminess while frozen berries add weight. Sometimes it is nice to add water, milk, soymilk, or nutmilk; each will affect the texture in different ways. Play around with different fruits, different liquids, and different proportions of frozen to unfrozen fruit until you find a fruit synergy and texture that suits your taste.

# Mango

Mango is the fruit of a tropical evergreen tree native to India. Mangoes are in the same plant family as poison ivy, and their skin contains oils that can produce allergic reactions in sensitive people. The flesh, however, is delicious and very versatile.

### STORAGE

· Unripe mango should not be refrigerated as the cold hampers the ripening process.

· Ripe mangoes will be slightly soft to the touch and should be refrigerated. They will keep for about a week.

### COOKING

· Ripe mangoes are usually eaten **raw**. Unripe mangoes are frequently **cooked** into stews and chutneys.

· Ripe mango mixes quite well with dairy and is frequently blended into smoothies. Mango has a creamy texture that lends itself to pulverization.

### HOW TO CUT A MANGO

· Mangoes have a large pit that runs through the center of the fruit. It is quite difficult to remove, so the fruit must be cut around it.

· Position the mango so that its stem faces you and the narrower side of the fruit is on the cutting board (such that if you let go of the mango it would roll over). The seed is now positioned parallel to how you will cut.

· Mango seeds are about a half inch thick and are shaped like a flat mango in the very center of the fruit. Make two slightly off center cuts, slicing the mango into three pieces, two fruity pieces shaped like shells, and one cylindrical piece in the center with the seed embedded into it.

· The shell-shaped pieces can now be cut into strips, while more fruit can be cut away from the center.

· Make sure not to eat the peel!

### SYNERGIES

· Mangoes work very well with dairy because their skin already has a creamy texture. Try slicing mango into yogurt or blending it with yogurt milk and cardamom to make mango lassi.

· Underripe mangoes can complement meat quite nicely. Try stewing mango with red meat, coconut milk, onions, and ginger.

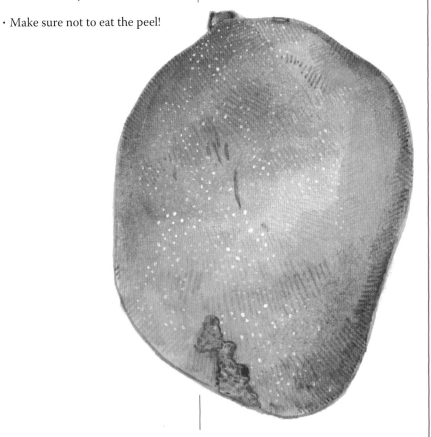

# Melon

Melons are a diverse group of large, ground-covering plants in the squash family. Honeydew and cantaloupe are members of the same Middle Eastern species and are colloquially known as muskmelons. Watermelon is closely related and native to southern Africa.

## STORAGE

· Melons will keep refrigerated for about two weeks or unrefrigerated (if they're too big to fit) for a few days.

· Melon should be opaque and pastel colored. If the color starts to deepen and become more transparent, cut that portion away to be composted. Melons usually start going bad on the portion closest to the stem, but they are so large that some sections are almost always salvageable.

## COOKING

· Melon should be eaten **raw** if at all possible, but processing methods like **juicing** or **boiling** into compote are useful if the melon is going bad.

· Melon skin should not be eaten, but eat as close to the skin as possible (even into the white rind on watermelons). The rind is crunchy and juicy and has lots of vitamins and minerals.

· **Juicing:** Watermelon makes excellent juice due to its high water content. Any juicing appliance will do.

## SYNERGIES

· Add some kick to watermelon juice by steeping it in ginger and mint. Try adding frozen berries instead of ice cubes.

· The size of most melons makes them the perfect base for fruit salads at large dinners.

### COMPOTE

To boil melon into compote, remove the rind, cut the flesh into pieces, and heat it in a pot on a medium heat for about half an hour. The sugar will caramelize and create a delicious compote, jam, or fruit sauce. An immersion blender can be used to speed up the process. Sugar can be added if desired.

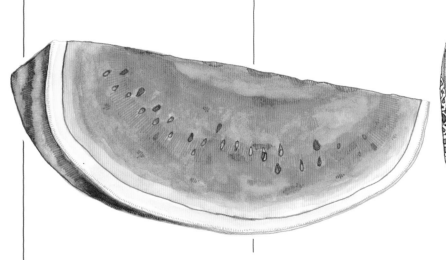

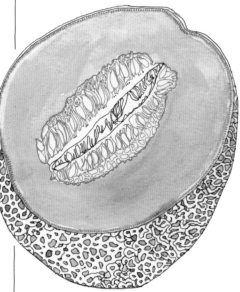

# Olives

Olives are the fruit of a flowering tree native to the Mediterranean. Olive trees can live more than 2,000 years. The olive fruits are hard and inedible when fresh—all olives are either processed into oil or fermented and cured before sale.

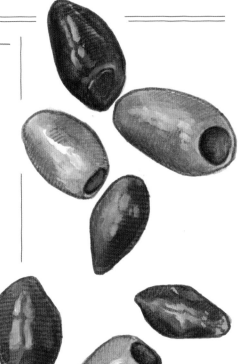

### STORAGE

· Because olives only come to market after they have been fermented and cured, olives can be stored unrefrigerated for over a year.

### COOKING

· Olives come preprocessed and do not need to be cooked. They can be eaten alone and are often used as a topping to add punctuation to a dish.

· Olives are extremely salty and slightly acidic. Think of them as the culinary equivalent of exclamation points!

### SYNERGIES

· Olives can add salt, flavor, and a little bit of fat to salads, so they help make the greens feel more substantial.

· Olives can add welcome intensity to pasta dishes.

· Try adding pitted olives to tomato sauce, hummus, or pesto.

### OLIVE OIL

· Olive oil is unique among plant based oils in that it comes from a fruit rather than a seed.

· As such, olive oil is much lighter and has a more complex flavor than many other oils.

· However, olive oil also burns very easily, and its flavor is easily marred by cooking. Heat olive oil as little as possible.

# Pears

Pears come from a flowering tree in the rose family native to the mountains of western China, but they spread naturally to foothill regions in most of Eurasia. Pear flesh contains small clusters of woody cells (called stone cells or grits) that give pears their unique coarse texture.

## STORAGE

· Ripe pears should be refrigerated and will last about two weeks.

· Keep unripe pears unrefrigerated. They will ripen faster if exposed to ethylene gas. To ripen especially quickly, put pears in an enclosed container with a banana.

· Some pear cultivars are crunchy when ripe; others are quite soft. The time to eat a pear is mostly based on personal preference.

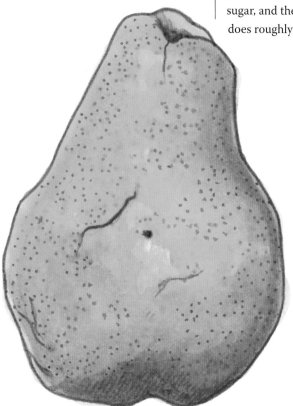

· Pears bruise very easily, but even extensive bruising does not ruin the fruit. Brown and slimy portions can be cut away.

## COOKING

· Ripe pears are best when eaten **raw**, but they can be **juiced** and are frequently **baked** in pastries or **cooked** into compote.

· Unripe pears are delicious when cooked. Ripening is mostly a process of transforming starch into sugar, and the heat from cooking does roughly the same conversion.

· To make pear compote, cut the flesh off the core and heat it in a soup pot on a medium heat for about half an hour. The sugar will caramelize and create a delicious compote, jam, or fruit sauce. An immersion blender can be used to speed up the process. Sugar can be added if desired.

## SYNERGIES

· Cooked pears make a great addition to oatmeal. Sauté them with a little butter for a couple of minutes and then mix them into cooked oatmeal for extra sweetness.

· Pears are sometimes nice to add to crunchy salads with lots of cucumbers and bell peppers and perhaps a bit of cheese.

# Pineapple

Pineapple is neither a pine nor an apple. Early explorers with little botanical knowledge named the fruit for its vague resemblance to a pinecone, but it is actually a plant from the Bromeliad family native to Central America.

### STORAGE

· Pineapple should be refrigerated and will keep for about a week.

· Ripe pineapple should be just slightly soft. Don't cut into it if it is too hard. Overripe pineapple is edible, but any uncut pineapple that is leaking juice should be composted.

### COOKING

· Pineapple is usually eaten **raw**, but it **juices** well and is sometimes **grilled** or **stir-fried**.

· Pineapple can be tricky to cut up. The outer skin is thickly textured—a lot of fruit is necessarily lost in the peeling process. Also, the inner core of a pineapple is quite hard and should be cut away.

· The inner core contains high quantities of an enzyme called bromelain that denatures protein. Bromelain is also present in the fruit in smaller amounts. Be careful when adding raw pineapple to dairy, as it may cause curdling. Cooking pineapple denatures the enzyme.

· Because of its bromelain content, pineapple is often grilled or stir-fried with meat. Bromelain works as a natural meat tenderizer.

### SYNERGIES

· Try grilling pineapple and serving it like tomato slices on burgers.

· Pineapple does well in fruit salads with melon or berries.

# Stone Fruits

Stone fruits—peaches, plums, cherries, apricots, nectarines, and so on—all belong to the same genus of tree called *Prunus*, part of the rose family. *Prunus* trees are famous for their spectacular flowerings in the early spring before their leaves have grown. The stone fruits are named for their large seeds (stones) that contain trace amounts of cyanide, but not enough to harm you.

### STORAGE

· Stone fruits should be refrigerated and will keep for several days.

· Stone fruits have thin, edible skins, which damage quite easily when the fruits are ripe. Handle them with care.

### COOKING

· Stone fruits are best eaten **raw** but are frequently **preserved** in fruit compote and can also be **juiced**.

· To make stone fruit compote, cut the flesh in half and remove the stones. Heat it in a soup pot on medium heat for about an hour. The sugar will caramelize and create a delicious compote, jam, or fruit sauce. An immersion blender can be used to speed up the process. Sugar can be added if desired but is rarely necessary since stone fruits are very sweet.

### SYNERGIES

· Stone fruits are a great addition to oatmeal and cereals.

· Try mixing slices of peach or cherry into yogurt with some nuts and vanilla.

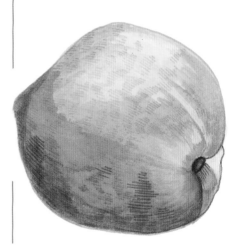

# Tomatoes

Tomatoes are a fruit in the nightshade family native to Mexico. Since their introduction to Europe and Asia 400 years ago, they have diversified tremendously and can be found in an array of shapes, sizes, colors, and flavors. They range from quite sweet to quite sour and so are one of the most versatile ingredients. A good tomato goes well with just about everything.

## STORAGE

· Fresh tomatoes usually need not be refrigerated, but older tomatoes that are cracked or have mushy spots should be kept in the fridge.

· Tomatoes should only be eaten fresh within a week of picking, but tomatoes will keep for cooking for about three weeks. Fresh and wrinkled tomatoes taste the same when cooked.

## COOKING

· Tomatoes can be **baked, roasted, juiced, stir-fried**, and **boiled** into soup, sauce, and stew. They are also great eaten **raw**.

· Tomato flavor varies quite a bit, but in general, small orange tomatoes are sweeter than larger red ones.

· **Cook time:** Cook time for tomatoes is variable since they can be eaten raw. The longer a tomato cooks, the less crisp it will be. Tomatoes transform from a fruit to a sauce through cooking.

### STIR-FRYING

· It's a good idea to cut tomatoes into chunks before cooking so that the juice spills out and coats the rest of your food.

· Tomatoes are great for adding moisture to the stir-fry without using too much water. They also add a subtle acidity that is impossible to attain with other acidic ingredients like sour citrus or vinegar.

## TOMATO SAUCE

### BOILING

· To make tomato sauce, cut tomatoes into large chunks and heat them in a large pot with vegetables, fats, and flavorers (mushrooms, eggplant, okra, bell pepper, zucchini, onions, garlic, salt, etc.).

· The sauce is done when the tomatoes disintegrate. It's a good idea to precook some of the vegetables in the sauce so that they finish when the tomatoes do.

### BAKING

· Tomato sauce can also be made by baking tomatoes on a high heat until the outsides begin to crack and brown and then blending them in a blender or food processor with flavoring vegetables, herbs, and spices.

· This method leaves the tomatoes tasting fresher than boiling them and also adds a great woody, roasted undertone. It's harder to add flavoring vegetables and other veggies with this method, though, since it's necessary to cook them separately and add them after blending.

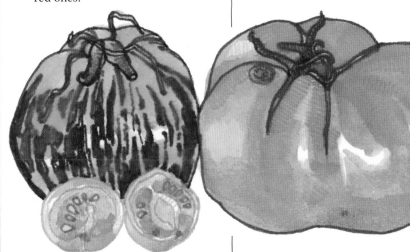

# dairy

● ⁑ ⁑ ⁑ ⁑ ⁑ ⁑ ●

**EVEN MORE THAN FRUIT,** dairy was designed specifically for you to eat it. Dairy is a special substance that is produced only by mammals. It is manufactured as milk in the mammary glands, for which mammals get their name. The milk we eat comes from three main species: cows, goats, and sheep. Milk is loaded with sugar, fat, and protein, perfect for a growing youngster. Despite its nutritional density, milk is often difficult for adults to digest. The reasons why are complex, but it is partially because milk is very species specific (cow's milk is meant for calves; people lack cow digestive enzymes) and partially because milk is very age specific (milk is meant for infants; adults lack baby digestive enzymes). Because milk is often difficult to process, and also because it spoils very easily, humans have devised many fermentation methods to preserve and predigest the dairy before we eat it. Cheese and yogurt are both fermented milk. Dairy is very nutritionally dense and high in calories. Like fruit, it makes a great snack on its own and requires little preparation. That said, it is also a very flexible cooking ingredient and can be added to nearly any dish to even out the flavor or add a bit of weight. Dairy makes dishes taste heartier.

# Cheese

Cheese is milk that has been fermented by fungi and bacteria. The diversity of cheeses available today reflects the diversity of fermentation methods, and fungal and bacterial species, that exist. Most cheese production requires rennet, a coagulating enzyme found in mammalian stomachs.

### STORAGE

· Cheese can be kept refrigerated for about a month.

· Hard cheeses can be frozen and will keep for about a year.

· Mold found on hard cheese can be cut away, and the rest of the cheese will remain good to eat. Mold can be eaten as well, although undesired mold is usually not that tasty. On the other hand, desired mold is central to the flavor of most cheese, especially brie and blue cheese.

### COOKING

· Cheese can be eaten **raw** but is also **baked** on top of food, **melted** into it, or mixed into a **stir-fry**.

· Cheese comes in hundreds of varieties. Each variety has its own quirks, consistency, melting temperature, and synergies with other foods. Some are better cooked, and some are better raw. Play around with different cheeses and experiment to find out for yourself what goes well with what.

· **Baking:** Cheese can be sprinkled over anything baked in the oven to add a cheesy flavor and crunchy crust. Mixing cheese into the dish before baking will bind everything together with deliciously melty goo.

· **Stir-frying:** Stir-frying cheese also has a melting effect. The cheese will cover the other ingredients and keep them stuck together.

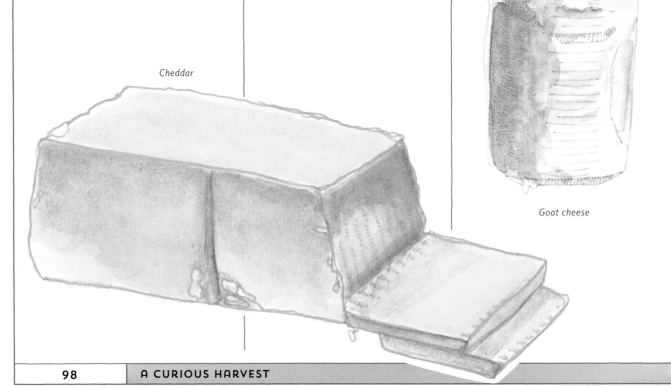

*Cheddar*

*Goat cheese*

## SYNERGIES

· Melted cheese will make dishes heartier and heavier.

· Cheese can be melted on toast to make a haphazard pizza. It also is an essential part of many sandwiches.

· Crumbled cheese goes great on salad.

· Cheese is often grated and sprinkled on top of hot dishes like pasta or soup so that it melts into them.

· Cheese scrambles wonderfully into eggs. It makes the eggs both fluffier and heartier.

· Cheese is a helpful binder in bean stews and curries. It adds richness and weight and helps balance out the more spicy flavors.

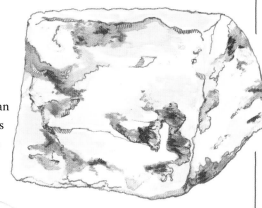

*Blue cheese*

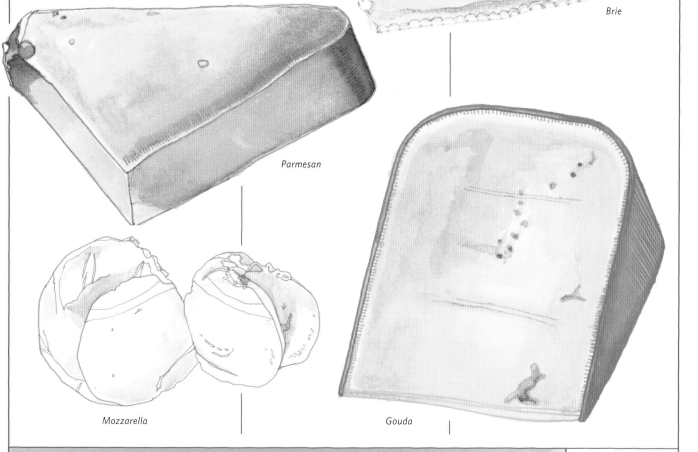

*Brie*

*Parmesan*

*Mozzarella*

*Gouda*

# Milk

The majority of the milk we drink today comes from cows. Cow's milk is usually pasteurized and homogenized to control disease and fat content. Goat's milk and sheep's milk can be found in specialty stores.

## STORAGE

· Milk must be refrigerated and will keep for about a week.

· Souring milk need not be poured down the drain. It won't make you sick; it just tastes different.

· Souring milk can be fermented into yogurt, or it can be added to soups to make them creamier and slightly tart.

## COOKING

· Milk is usually consumed **raw**, but it has a variety of culinary uses.

· Milk can be used instead of water in many dishes to make the food heartier and creamier.

· Add milk to soup to thicken the broth.

· Milk can be added to overly spicy food to balance out the flavor.

· Milk is naturally high in sugar, so it tends to go better with sweet palates.

## SYNERGIES

· Try making a sweet squash soup with honey and ginger that uses a mixture of milk and water for broth.

· Boil oatmeal with milk instead of water. Also try boiling a grain like rice or bulgur wheat in milk with sweeteners to make porridge.

· Adding milk to scrambled eggs will make the eggs fluffier and heartier.

· Milk is a great addition to potatoes, sweet potatoes, and other starchy roots. It adds moisture and weight.

· Milk can be frothed with a blender, immersion blender, or food processor to make a delicious foam for drinks. Milk with a high fat content works best.

# Yogurt

Yogurt is made by fermenting milk with multiple species of bacteria. Eating yogurt helps modulate the bacterial populations in your gut, which can be damaged by poor diet and antibiotic use.

## HOW TO MAKE YOGURT

· To make yogurt, all you need is milk and a spoonful of yogurt. The spoonful of yogurt acts as a starter culture to seed the fermentation of the rest of the milk.

· The quality of milk is very important. Try to use milk with a high fat content.

· **Heat:** To start the fermentation process, heat milk on the stove to about 180°F (82°C). Then, let it cool to about the temperature of a too hot bath—the temperature bacteria like to grow in.

· **Inoculate:** Pour the milk into a large jar with a sealing lid and add a spoonful of yogurt. Mix the yogurt in thoroughly.

· **Ferment:** Put the jar in a warm place to ferment overnight. Try an oven that is just barely turned on, or a cooler filled with hot water. Leaving the yogurt next to a heater also works.

· **Eat:** The next morning, the yogurt will be ready to eat! You may want to chill your yogurt before using it.

· **Filter:** If the yogurt is too watery, you can filter the water out with cheesecloth. The water that is removed is called whey. It tastes slightly sour and is full of protein. Whey can be used as a base for soup. The remaining solids on top will be a thicker yogurt.

## STORAGE

· Yogurt should be kept refrigerated and will keep for a few weeks.

## COOKING

· Yogurt is usually eaten **raw**, but it also has a variety of culinary uses.

· Yogurt is partially digested milk. It contains significantly less lactose than milk does (the bacteria eat it all), so it is much easier for our bodies to process. Yogurt can be used as a milk substitute in most dishes.

· Yogurt can be added to soups to make them richer and creamier. It can also be used to balance out overly spicy stews.

· Yogurt is naturally high in sugar, and so it tends to go better with sweet palates. That said, it is also quite sour, and will make whatever you add it to taste tart.

· Yogurt can be frozen into frozen yogurt. Simply add sweeteners and toss it into the freezer. The trick to making good frozen yogurt is to make sure the yogurt freezes very slowly. If it freezes too quickly, you'll just get a frozen brick that can't be eaten. To prevent this, take the yogurt out of the freezer about once an hour and give it a good stir to break up all the large ice crystals into smaller ones. If you do this several times, all the yogurt will freeze into tiny unattached ice crystals that can be easily scooped.

## SYNERGIES

· Adding yogurt to scrambled eggs will make the eggs fluffier and heartier.

· Yogurt is a great addition to potatoes, sweet potatoes, and other starchy roots. It adds moisture and weight.

· Try complementing plain yogurt with a mixture of fruit, nuts, sweeteners, and flavorers like cinnamon, clove, or vanilla.

# fats

CONTRARY TO POPULAR BELIEF, fats are not bad for you, even the saturated kinds. Fats are the most energy-dense food you can eat, and they aid in the digestion of many important vitamins. Fats vary in size and composition, but they all have a skeleton made from long chains of carbon, with a skin of hydrogen surrounding the carbon backbone. Sometimes the carbon skeleton contains a double bond, which causes the molecule to bend and take up more space. These doubly bonded, bended fats are said to be unsaturated, whereas straight fats made up of just singly bonded carbons are called saturated fats. Straight, saturated fats pack together efficiently, so they are solid at room temperature. The bent, unsaturated fats don't fit together as nicely, so they remain liquid at room temperature. This liquid-solid, unsaturated-saturated difference accounts for the differences between butter and oil. Fats are difficult to digest, and saturated fats are harder to process than the unsaturated kind, so they should only be eaten in small quantities. That said, fats are absolutely essential to a healthy diet and cooking would be impossible without them. It is a good idea to add a small amount of fat to almost anything you cook. The fat provides lubrication between the food and the cooking surface so your ingredients don't burn. Additionally, the fat helps bring out flavors in your cooking that otherwise would not be present. It's good to use fats in moderation, but don't underestimate their value.

# Animal Fat

Animal fats are saturated fats with distinctly meaty flavors. Popular opinion holds that they are unhealthy, but in fact they are more palatable and easier to digest than the manufactured saturated fats like hydrogenated soybean and corn oil.

## STORAGE

· Animal fat can be stored unrefrigerated for several weeks.

## PREPARATION

· Animal fat can be derived from unwanted meat products like chicken carcasses and leftover sparerib bones.

· Place the bones and meat in a large pot and fill it with water.

· Boil the water for a couple of hours. The animal fat will melt and float to the surface.

· Slowly pour the fat off the surface when it is liquid or wait for the water to cool at which point the solid layer of fat can be lifted off the top with a fork. The fat can be stored unrefrigerated for many weeks.

· Filter out the boiled bones. The remaining broth makes an excellent soup stock or can be used to boil rice or beans to add extra flavor. See Vegetable Stock, page 118.

· Bacon is a very easy source of animal fat. Simply pour the liquid fat into a glass after cooking.

## COOKING

· Animal fat has a very strong flavor and will make whatever you cook in it taste like meat.

· Unlike store-bought oils, animal fat will contain a lot of impurities, so it tends to burn if left on high heat. Don't use it for frying.

· Animal fat is great for cooking eggs, beans, and meat. It also works well with vegetable stir-fries, if you want meat-flavored vegetables.

## SYNERGIES

· Try sauteing a mixture of carrots, beets, parsnips, or other root vegetables in bacon fat.

· Some baked goods, especially savory scones or biscuits, are especially tasty when butter is replaced with animal fat.

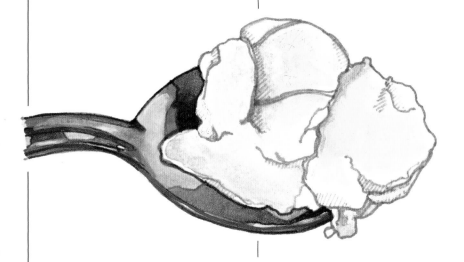

# Butter and Cream

Butter and cream are fat products derived from dairy. Because dairy is high in sugar, these fats are well suited for baked products and other sweet dishes. Their flavor is mild but quite distinct and usually superior to vegetable fats.

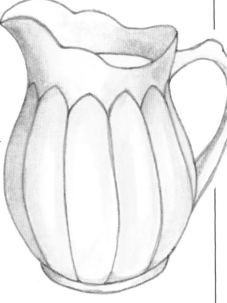

### BUTTER

Butter is made by isolating the fat content of milk from the rest of the liquid. This is done by churning and agitating the milk until the diffuse fat binds together and rises to the top.

### STORAGE

· Butter can be stored unrefrigerated for over a week.

· Leaving butter out of the fridge is a nice way to keep it soft. It won't go rancid, but it might melt on hot days.

### COOKING

· Butter has a rich and unique flavor. It is particularly suited for grains, especially bread and pasta.

· Butter burns quite easily—avoid cooking it on high heat.

### CREAM

Cream is a milk product produced in a way very similar to butter, by churning and skimming the fat from the top. But unlike butter, which is close to 100 percent fat, cream is more like fatty milk and usually contains about 30 percent fat.

### STORAGE

· Cream should be refrigerated. Its high fat content lets it keep longer than milk, for about two weeks.

### COOKING

· Cream can be used to add weight and richness to soups or baked goods.

· To make whipped cream, mix cream in a blender or food processor for about ten minutes. Sweeteners and spices make the cream heavier and harder to whip, so add them at the end.

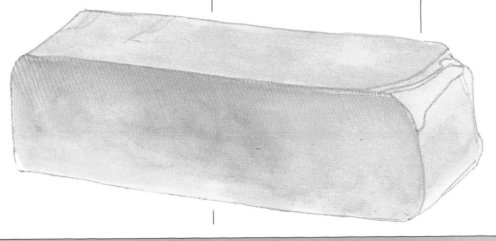

# Vegetable Oils

Vegetable oils are typically liquid at room temperature, as they are unsaturated fats. They tend to have less-distinct flavors than animal fats as they have a simpler chemical makeup. Their purity allows vegetable oils to withstand very high heats without burning. All high-temperature cooking, especially deep-frying, should be done with vegetable oils.

**Coconut oil** carries more flavor than most oils. It's best used with food that is not spiced very heavily so the coconut can be tasted.

**Sesame oil** is a very dark oil that tastes distinctly of nutty sesame. Use it in stir-fries to add some earthy tones.

**Olive oil** contains a multitude of delicate flavors. Use it on salads or food that is cooked only briefly so that its subtle taste doesn't get cooked away.

**Canola oil** is a wonderful general-purpose oil. It has little to no flavor and contains higher concentrations of fatty acids than other oils.

**Sunflower oil** is flavorless and is great for frying.

**Soybean oil** is cheaper than most other oils and is useful for frying.

**Corn oil** is likely the cheapest cooking oil. It is also one of the most highly processed. Use it for frying.

**Grapeseed oil** is a by-product of the wine-making process. It is useful for frying.

## STORAGE

· Vegetable oils can be kept unrefrigerated for several years.

## COOKING

### TO MAKE A STIR-FRY

· Coat the bottom of the pan with a thin layer of oil.

· As you mix in vegetables and other ingredients, the oil will lightly coat everything and enhance the flavors.

· Make sure not to add too much oil—excess oil easily overwhelms the dish and is hard to digest.

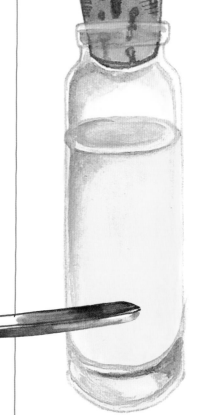

## TO FRY FOOD

· Fill a pan with about half an inch (1 cm) of high-temperature oil.

· Heat the pan for about ten minutes. Don't add food until the oil is quite hot.

· Add your ingredients and let them sizzle.

· Flip them over when the sides turn golden brown.

· When ingredients are done, remove them and put them on a plate with some paper towels to absorb the excess oil.

## SYNERGIES

· Add a little bit of oil to boiling grains to keep them from sticking to the bottom of the pot.

· Adding a bit of oil to soup can improve the flavor tremendously.

· Very nice olive oil can be used instead of butter on bread and is a great addition to salad dressing.

· In general, add oil to dishes that you don't want to be too dry but don't want to add water to.

## COOKING TEMPERATURES

The most important thing to keep in mind when cooking with oil is its smoking threshold. Some oils will smoke at high temperatures, making the food taste smoky and setting off fire alarms. To prevent this, only fry food with high-temperature oils.

Here is a list of fats in order of ideal cooking temperatures, lowest to highest.

Animal fat

Butter

Coconut oil

Olive oil

Sesame oil

HOTER

*Above this line, the fat will start to smoke if left on high heat. Below this line, burning risk is reduced.*

Canola oil

Sunflower oil

Soybean oil

Corn oil

Grapeseed oil

# flavorers

●∴∴∴∴∴∴∴●

THIS BOOK (somewhat artificially) divides the ingredients we use to add extra flavor to our meals into four major categories: flavoring vegetables, spices, herbs, and sweeteners. Flavorers don't add much nutritional value, but the nuance they provide is essential. Good cooks distinguish themselves by their use of flavorers. Every culture in the world cooks with similar combinations of vegetables, carbohydrates, and proteins, and it is mostly through unique uses of flavorers that distinct cooking styles emerge. All flavorers are used in small quantities, but even in minute portions, flavorers have a disproportionate effect on the taste of a dish. Flavorers are all quite distinct—it is very difficult to describe most tastes in words—and the number of possible flavors they can produce when combined is essentially infinite. A cook's skill can be measured by their ability to select the most pleasing combinations from this infinite array. Skillful use of flavorers requires a willingness to experiment, and it is quite easy to teach yourself. Try some unorthodox combinations. You will be pleasantly surprised!

# flavoring vegetables

● ┼ ┼ ●

**FLAVORING VEGETABLES** are fresh vegetables that are cooked with in fairly large quantities. But because they add such a distinct flavor to the food, they are better considered as a kind of spice rather than as a central ingredient. In fact, all of the flavorful vegetables listed in this book can be found in dried and powdered forms in jars on grocery store shelves. It is much preferable to use fresh flavoring vegetables if at all possible, although the dried forms will do in a pinch. Flavoring vegetables are usually chopped very finely and added to a dish at the very beginning of cooking, so that their flavor suffuses the other ingredients. The cook time of flavoring vegetables can be varied, with shorter cook times producing stronger, harsher flavors and longer times producing milder, subtler, and more complex flavors. Flavoring vegetables are an essential base in most dishes.

# Garlic

Garlic is a bulb plant in the onion family native to the mountains of Central Asia. Garlic cloves are enlarged leaf buds in which the plant stores its nutrients over winter so it can produce leaves in the spring. Garlic is packed with preservative chemicals that protect it from pests and is said to be good for your immune system.

## STORAGE

· Garlic can be stored unrefrigerated for over a month.

· Garlic rarely actually rots—it usually just gets a little brown and dries out. Dried brown garlic can still be added to soups.

## PEELING

· To peel a head of garlic quickly, separate the cloves and put them in a small (preferably metal) bowl. Place another bowl on top and shake the container vigorously for about a minute. With enough agitation, the skin will separate from the cloves.

· Another method is to cut the base off of each clove and then crush it with a knife. After crushing, the clove easily separates from the peel.

## COOKING

· Garlic can be eaten **raw**, or it can be **stir-fried**, **baked**, **roasted**, or **boiled**.

· **Cook time:** Garlic's flavor varies dramatically with cook time. Raw or lightly cooked garlic is spicy and peppery, while cooked garlic becomes milder and creamier.

· **Stir-frying:** In stir-fries with garlic, experiment with oil levels and cook times to change the strength of the flavor.

· **Raw:** Raw garlic can be crushed or puréed in a food processor and mixed with oil, salt, and herbs to make a strong sauce or spread like aioli or pesto.

· **Baked:** Garlic cloves can be baked whole and have a rich, almost sweet flavor and a texture similar to potato.

· **Boiling:** Garlic goes great in soups and can be boiled whole or diced finely.

· Garlic skins go great in soup stock.

## SYNERGIES

· Garlic goes well in almost any dish that isn't sweet.

· Garlic goes well with most vegetables. Chop it finely and mix it into stir-fries or soups.

· Garlic complements most carbohydrates, but it is particularly suited to potatoes. Garlic cloves can be roasted whole with potatoes and then mashed with them.

# Ginger

Ginger is a rhizomatous plant native to India. The ginger "root" we eat is actually a rhizome, a horizontally growing underground stem. Ginger has long been touted as a folk remedy for all sorts of digestive troubles; it contains compounds that were recently shown to bind to digestive neurons in the gut.

## STORAGE

· Ginger can be stored unrefrigerated and will keep for over a month.

· Ginger can be frozen and will keep for over a year.

## PEELING

· Ginger is usually peeled, but this isn't always a necessity. If the ginger is fresh and the peel is clean, it can be chopped and cooked just like the ginger flesh.

· Ginger can be peeled with a vegetable peeler, but scraping the skin with a spoon or butter knife also works well.

· Ginger peels go great in soup stock.

· Frozen ginger is easier to peel than fresh ginger, but the flavor of frozen ginger is weaker than fresh.

## COOKING

· Ginger can be **stir-fried**, **baked**, **roasted**, **boiled**, **juiced**, **candied**, and made into **tea**.

· **Stir-frying:** When stir-frying ginger, be mindful to dice it quite finely. Most people dislike large chunks of ginger in their food. (I am not one of them.)

· Diced ginger goes great in soups and stews. It can also be baked with meat or squash.

· **Tea:** Ginger can be boiled with its peel on into tea. Alternatively, the flesh can be used for cooking and the peels can be boiled into tea separately. Be careful not to boil ginger tea for too long—a few minutes is fine; after several minutes, the tea can become quite peppery.

· **Juice:** Ginger can be juiced in a commercial juicer. Its juice is extremely potent and adds a nice kick to fruit juice.

## CANDIED

· To make candied ginger, boil peeled chunks of ginger for a long time.

· Once the ginger is soft and most of the water is gone, add a whole lot of sugar (about as much sugar as there is ginger). Boil the ginger, water, and sugar mixture together.

· After the sugar has had some time to be absorbed by the ginger, strain the ginger out of the syrup.

· The syrup can be diluted later into a sweet ginger tea.

· While the ginger is still hot and sticky, put it in a bowl and mix in a few handfuls of sugar until the ginger is nicely coated with white crystals. This ginger candy will likely be much stronger than store bought.

## SYNERGIES

· Ginger is one of the few spices that work well with both a sweet and spicy palate. It is exceptionally versatile and tastes good with almost everything. It is an excellent flavorer to experiment with.

· Ginger is suited to most vegetables, especially the sweeter ones like squash or carrots.

· Try stir-frying meat in a marinade of ginger and soy sauce.

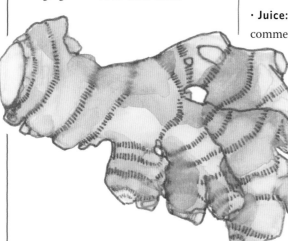

# Horseradish

Horseradish is an extremely pungent root vegetable in the Brassica family native to the Mediterranean. Like other brassicas, horseradish leaves are edible when cooked. This is not frequently done, however, because horseradish leaves taste like horseradish. Ironically, horseradish is reported to be poisonous to horses.

## STORAGE

· Whole horseradish can be stored unrefrigerated and will keep for several months.

· The flavorful compounds in horseradish break down quite quickly when exposed to air. After grating, use horseradish immediately or store it submerged in oil or vinegar to keep it away from oxygen. This method has the added benefit of flavoring the oil or vinegar for later use.

## PEELING

· Fresh horseradish is often quite gnarled and has a very thick skin. A vegetable peeler may be insufficient, so a sharp knife should be used to cut away the thick outer layer.

## COOKING

· Horseradish is quite strong and should be used sparingly. It can be **baked, roasted**, **stir-fried**, or **boiled** into soup or stew.

· Grated horseradish, oil, and vinegar can be mixed into a very creamy emulsion. Use it as a sauce for stir-fries or as a salad dressing.

## SYNERGIES

· Try frying fish with vinegar, horseradish, and some salt.

· Mixing a bit of horseradish into mashed potatoes can add a nice kick.

· Try stir-frying leafy greens with a mixture of chopped horseradish and ginger.

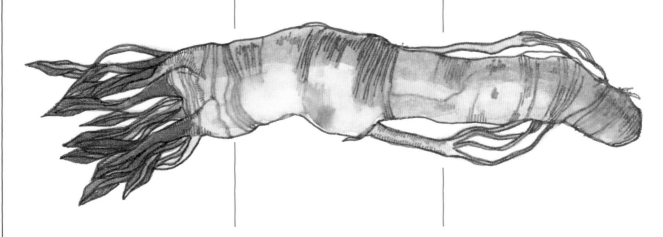

# Hot Peppers

Hot peppers are the fruits of a group of shrubby plants in the nightshade family native to Mexico. Most varieties are the same biological species as bell peppers but have been bred to contain greatly increased quantities of capsaicin, which gives them their hot and spicy flavor.

## STORAGE

· Fresh hot peppers should be refrigerated, where they will last for several weeks.

· Hot peppers are frequently dried and can last for several years, although potency declines with age.

## COOKING

· Hot peppers can be **stir-fried**, **baked**, **roasted**, **boiled** into soup or stew, and can be made into **hot sauce**.

· **Cook time:** Spiciness varies greatly from pepper to pepper, and it also varies with cook time. Hot peppers are spiciest before they have been heated. Extensive cooking will make hot peppers milder. Some hot peppers are incredibly potent, and just one is enough to make a dish almost painful to eat.

· If a dish is too hot, sweeteners or dairy (either milk, yogurt, or cheese) can be added to reduce the spiciness and even out the flavors.

· When cutting hot peppers, be mindful of your fingernails. Juice that finds its way under the nail can cause irritation for several hours.

· Hot pepper seeds and ends are great to add to soup stock.

## HOT SAUCE

· There are many ways to make hot sauce, but all methods involve blending hot peppers with salt, sugar, vinegar, or other flavorers like garlic or onion. Here's how to make hot sauce:

· Purée a mixture of hot peppers and other flavorers in a blender or food processor.

· This puree can be used as a condiment raw, or . . .

· Simmer the purée on the stove for a few minutes to homogenize the mixture and even out the flavor.

· Alternatively, it might be preferable to roast the hot peppers and other flavoring vegetables in the oven first before blending them. Roasting allows the peppers to blend much more easily so simmering isn't necessary. Roasted hot sauce tends to be creamier than raw or simmered.

· Virtually every ingredient in hot sauce is used as a preservative for other foods, so hot sauce has a very long shelf life. It will last for many months in a refrigerated jar.

## SYNERGIES

· Boil beans with one or two hot peppers. Don't forget to take the pepper out or at least dice it up before serving.

· Try blending hot peppers into hummus, guacamole, or pesto. Bake it beforehand to even out the flavor a bit.

· Hot peppers are a great addition to tomato sauce.

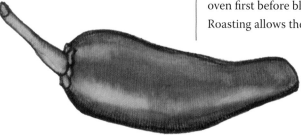

# Onions

Onions are a diverse group of bulbous plants native to the mountains of Central Asia. Onion bulbs are formed as the plant stores excess nutrients in the base of its leaves over winter so it can produce new shoots in the coming spring. Onions come in many shapes, sizes, and names. Chives, shallots, leeks, and scallions are all forms of onion with similar flavors and cooking requirements.

### STORAGE

· Onion bulbs can be kept unrefrigerated and will last for about a month.

· Onion bulbs grow in layers, so they are easy to salvage. If one or two layers are brown and slimy, simply peel them off. In most cases, there will be a pristine layer underneath.

· Sometimes older onions begin to sprout. This is perfectly fine; the green shoot is just as tasty as the bulb.

### COOKING

· Onion bulbs can be **stir-fried, baked, roasted, grilled**, or **boiled** into soups or stews.

· As onions cook, their flavor becomes milder. Cooking onions release a lot of water and lose most of their volume. They eventually disintegrate completely, leaving a trace of fiber and a lovely flavor.

· **Cook time:** It's not really possible to overcook onions, but if you want your onions to taste stronger or have more of a crunch, only cook them for a brief period of time.

· Different onion cultivars vary greatly in how pungent they are and also in their sugar content. Many onions are quite sweet and stir-fry nicely with apples.

### SYNERGIES

· Onions go well in a huge variety of dishes. It's never a bad idea to set some onions sizzling in a little bit of oil as the first step to a meal.

· Raw onion is sometimes nice to add to dips and spreads blended in a food processor, like pesto or hummus.

· Try baking onions with root vegetables and tofu.

· Onions go great in meat and vegetable stir-fries.

# Green Onions

Green onions taste the same as bulb onions, but they are less pungent and more leafy and delicate. Some onion cultivars, like leeks and chives, are grown specially for their flavorful leaves, but even the leaves of white onion bulbs can be cooked with.

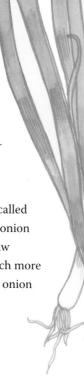

## STORAGE

· Green onion leaves should be refrigerated.

· Leeks will last for several weeks, but the greens of chives, scallions, or any other cultivar with loose leaves will only last a few days.

· If the onion bulb has a much larger diameter than the leaves, it's a good idea to separate them from each other and cook them separately. The bulb will last for much longer.

## COOKING

· Green onion leaves can be **stir-fried**, **boiled** into soups or stews, or served **raw** as a garnish.

· **Cook time:** Green onion leaves are much milder than the onion bulb, and it is quite possible to overcook them. Onion greens are well cooked when they soften and their color changes to a deep, vibrant green. Stop cooking them well before their color starts to fade.

· The more delicate onion leaves like chives need not be cooked at all and are best sprinkled over a soup, stew, or stir-fry just before cooking is completed.

· Leeks require substantially longer cook times than other kinds of green onions. They exist on the surprisingly fuzzy border between onion bulbs and leaves.

## SYNERGIES

· Green onion leaves are a nice garnish for protein-rich soups. Cut them finely and stir them in close to the end of cooking.

· Green onions are well suited to scrambled eggs. The leaves can be tossed into the pan with the egg and add delightful green color and onion flavor without overwhelming the dish.

· In salads and dips where raw onion is called for, try to use green onion leaves if possible. Raw onion leaves are much more palatable than a raw onion bulb.

# Turmeric

Turmeric is a rhizomatous plant native to India. As a rhizome, turmeric grows underground but is actually a stem. It is in the ginger family and is said to be good for joint health.

## STORAGE

· Turmeric can be kept refrigerated for several weeks.

· Turmeric can be left unrefrigerated but will tend to dry out and become difficult to cook with.

## COOKING

· Turmeric can be **stir-fried, baked, roasted,** or **boiled** into soup.

· Turmeric has a subtle earthy and yet fresh flavor and a remarkably vibrant yellow color that tends to stain anything else you cook it with.

· **Cook time:** Turmeric produces a spectrum of color from neon yellow to orange-brown depending on cook time and the original color of the food. Shorter cook times produce neon yellow, which turns to orange and then brown with increased exposure to heat.

## SYNERGIES

· Use turmeric as a food coloring on anything that looks brown or pale. Its mild flavor allows it to mix well with almost anything, but its color makes it especially suited for white foods like cauliflower, poultry, fennel, or rice.

· Turmeric is a fantastic addition to hummus—it adds vibrant color to an otherwise plain-looking spread.

· Add turmeric to chicken soup to color both the meat and the broth.

### POWDERED OR FRESH?

· With most flavoring vegetables, given a choice between fresh and dried powders, the best choice is fresh, hands down—except for turmeric.

· Fresh turmeric is nice—it has a unique springy earthy flavor that can nicely complement grains or beans—but sometimes turmeric flavor is not desired but its yellow color is.

· Powdered turmeric actually confers a stronger coloring effect than fresh turmeric does. Dry turmeric is close to tasteless, so it can be used almost exclusively as food coloring.

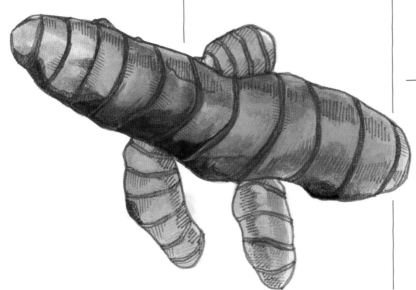

# Vegetable Stock

Vegetable stock is a broth made from the unwanted portions of vegetables.
Making vegetable stock is a great way to get the most out of your ingredients.
It reduces waste and extracts extra minerals and flavors from your veggies.

## PREPARATION

· Collect all discarded vegetable scraps in a large pot.

· Here are some examples:

  - The tops and bottoms of carrot, parsnip, beet, eggplant, tomato, bell pepper, zucchini, fennel, and celery

  - Wilting leafy greens, unwanted stems, and leaves from herbs and veggies

  - The skins of garlic, onion, ginger, turmeric, horseradish, and kohlrabi

  - Bay leaves

  - Any and all vegetable scraps will do.

· Fill the pot with water and boil it for at least two hours. Strain out the vegetables, and a rich brown broth will be left.

· You can boil meat scraps and bones in vegetable stock as well. (See Animal Fat on page 104.) Keep in mind that meat stock goes rancid faster than vegetable stock.

## STORAGE

· If you don't have enough vegetable scraps to merit making stock but don't want to throw them away, put them in a large jar in the freezer. When the jar fills up, empty it out and make stock. Freezing won't affect the flavor.

· Vegetable stock can be stored unrefrigerated in sealed jars and will keep for over a week. It will last for over a month if refrigerated.

## COOKING

· Use vegetable stock instead of water in any dish where the water is consumed or absorbed by the food.

## SYNERGIES

· Boiled grains—Boil grains in vegetable stock instead of water to add extra flavor.

· Beans—Vegetable stock can add extra flavor to beans as well.

· Soup and stew—Use vegetable stock instead of water as a base for all soups and stews.

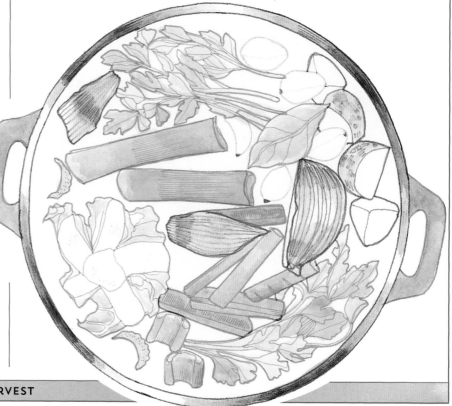

# sweeteners

●┄┼┄┼┄●

**SWEETENERS ARE,** simply put, any ingredient that contains sugar. The dominant substance in any sweetener will be sugar, and the dominant flavor will be sweet, but all sweeteners are not created equal. Sweeteners come from a variety of sources, and each source has unique qualities. Sweeteners can be mixed together and used interchangeably, but it is good to keep in mind their unique sources and subtle differences in flavor. A small change in the taste of a sweetener can go a long way. Five common sweeteners are outlined on the following pages.

# Table Sugar

Most white table sugar comes from sugarcane grass, but sugar is derived from other plants as well, notably beets. The same product can come from such different plants because table sugar is heavily processed to the point where it is basically pure glucose. The brown hue of all other sweeteners indicates the presence of minerals and plant matter that is processed out of white table sugar. Because of this processing, table sugar is lower in minerals and has a simpler flavor than all the other sweeteners.

### COOKING

· Because table sugar is so highly processed, it has basically no complex flavors and is 100 percent sweet. Use it in dishes where you want to add sweetness and don't care too much about the subtleties.

# Honey

Honey is derived from flower nectar and is harvested by bees. The bees process this nectar in their hive, dehydrating it and imbuing it with pollen, enzymes, and antibiotics that protect the honey from bacteria and other pests. The bees' labor gives honey a complex flavor with many positive health effects.

### STORAGE

· Honey can be stored unrefrigerated for several months.

· After a few months, honey will crystallize and become difficult to work with. Crystallized honey can be revitalized by heating it in a microwave or placing the honey jar in a pot of water and boiling for a few minutes.

### COOKING

· Honey has a very multifaceted flavor due to the unique way in which it was made. Enzymes, pollen, and an ever-changing array of flower nectars all contribute to the way honey tastes—and its flavor varies considerably from hive to hive.

· Honey is best used in dishes where its flavor can be appreciated in detail. It is quite viscous, so unlike maple syrup and agave, it will only dissolve quickly in warm liquids.

· Honey's viscosity makes it an excellent bread spread.

# Maple Syrup

Maple syrup comes from the sap of maple trees. In the early spring, the sap flowing up from the roots is harvested from the trees. Then much of the water is boiled off, leaving a brown syrup.

### COOKING

· Maple syrup is typically relegated to the realm of pancakes and waffles, but it can be used to add maple hints in any dish that lacks sweetness. Its consistency allows it to mix very easily with liquids and yogurt.

# Molasses

Molasses is a thick, brown-to-black syrup that is extracted from sugarcane before it is refined into table sugar crystals. Molasses is mostly sugar, but it also has other organic matter mixed in, which gives molasses its strong color and distinctive, slightly bitter flavor. Don't be fooled by brown sugar advertised as "natural." Sugar processors mix molasses back into refined white sugar and call it brown. Brown sugar is more expensive because you are paying for the process of removing and then reinfusing the sugar with plant matter.

### COOKING

· Molasses bears a wonderful combination of sweet and bitter flavors. It is mostly sweet but has a slightly bitter aftertaste, which gives it a nice kick.

· Molasses is a thick syrup that works great as a bread spread.

· Use molasses to add darker hints to dishes that might otherwise be overwhelmingly sweet.

# Agave

Agave is a sweetener harvested from the agave plant, a large succulent plant native to Mexico. Tequila is distilled from fermented agave.

### COOKING

· Agave is a syrup that is more viscous than maple syrup but less viscous than honey or molasses. It mixes well with liquids and yogurt.

# spices

●┼┼●

**SPICES ARE A DIVERSE GROUP** of ingredients that are used in small quantities to add flavor and texture to food. Many are derived from seeds, but cinnamon comes from bark, cloves from flower buds, and salt is not even of botanical origin. In general, a spice is any substance that is used to add flavor or texture. As a rule, spices don't need to be refrigerated. Spices will stay flavorful on the shelf for many years. More than any other ingredient type, using spices effectively requires creativity and a spirit of experimentation, as well as nonattachment to any particular outcome. Many spice mixtures will produce unexpected flavors, but unexpected does not equate with bad. Intuition can lead us to some delightful places if we give it a chance. Add a pinch of an unfamiliar spice or two to your food and see what happens!

# Cardamom

Cardamom is derived from the seeds of a small plant in the ginger family native to India. It is most commonly used in Middle Eastern and Indian cooking, but its nutty flavor is very versatile and is utilized by cultures all over the globe.

## FORMS

· Cardamom is sold as whole seed pods, loose seeds, and ground seeds.

· The seed pods can be problematic because they add unwanted coarse fibers to your food, and powdered seeds tend to lose their flavor after a while, so loose seeds are preferable.

· It's best to grind a small amount of cardamom seed in a coffee grinder and use the powder within a few days—fresh powder tastes best and flavors food evenly. But loose seeds can also be cooked with as is and will add a pungent kick of flavor when they are chewed.

## COOKING

· Cardamom is one of the few flavorers that work well with both a sweet and savory palate. Its flavor is very rich and earthy and slightly nutty. It is extremely flexible.

· A subtle hint of cardamom is pleasant in most dishes, but it very quickly can become overpowering. Use only a pinch of powder in most cases.

· When frying or stir-frying, add whole cardamom seeds to the oil as it is heating up. The flavorful compounds in cardamom are fat soluble, so frying the seeds is a great way to get the most flavor out of them.

## SYNERGIES

· Cardamom powder is nice to add to stir-fries, stews, and soups.

· Try grinding and brewing cardamom with coffee to give the drink a more complex flavor.

· Cardamom is a surprisingly excellent addition to desserts like baked goods and fruit salads. It can add welcome flavor diversity to dishes that would otherwise be homogenously sweet.

· The best use of whole cardamom pods is to boil them with grains. They will impart their flavor to the grain and are large and colorful enough to be easily removed before eating. Don't use whole cardamom pods in dishes where they might accidentally be eaten.

# Cinnamon

Cinnamon is derived from the bark of an evergreen tree native to India. Cinnamon is the only popular food that is derived directly from tree bark. Cinnamon has a long history as part of the ancient spice trade.

## FORMS

· Cinnamon comes in rolled-up strips of bark (sticks) and powder.

· Powder is usually preferable because it imparts flavor more efficiently than the sticks, which need to be removed from food before eating.

## COOKING

· Cinnamon tastes slightly sweet and nutty in small quantities and becomes rather spicy and hot in large amounts.

· Add powdered cinnamon to anything that tastes sweet. Cinnamon itself adds a kind of sweetness, so cinnamon powder can be used as a partial sugar substitute.

· Cinnamon sticks are best added to boiling dishes. Add cinnamon sticks to sweet porridges like oatmeal, fruit compote, or applesauce while they are cooking. Remove the sticks before eating.

## SYNERGIES

· Stir a bit of cinnamon into yogurt to add sweetness without sugar.

· Sprinkle a little cinnamon on baking squash.

· Try adding cinnamon to pancake or muffin batter.

· Cinnamon can be used minimally in stir-fries with sweet vegetables, like bell peppers, onions, and carrots.

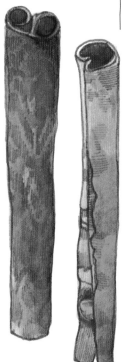

# Cloves

Cloves are the dried, immature flower buds of an evergreen tree native to a small archipelago in Indonesia. Clove trees can live for hundreds of years, and for most of ancient history, their location was closely guarded by spice traders seeking to maintain their monopoly.

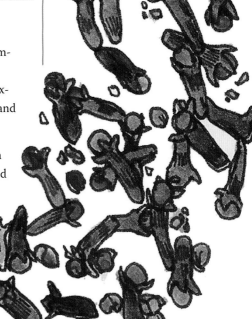

### FORMS

· Clove buds come whole or ground.

· Whole cloves retain their flavor much better than powder and can be ground in a coffee grinder when powder is desired.

### COOKING

· Cloves are very strong, so more than a pinch is usually unnecessary.

· Cloves are typically used for sweet things, like pastries and fruit dishes, but they sometimes add a nice balance to savory things, especially when there are onions involved.

### SYNERGIES

· Cloves can be ground and brewed with coffee to add complexity to the flavor.

· A pinch of clove in fruit salad or dessert dishes can add earthy highlights.

· Try adding a little bit of clove to a dish that uses a lot of onions.

· Cookie dough or French toast batter can be vastly improved by a pinch of clove.

### CLOVE HISTORY

· In the past, spice trade dominated global commerce, as spices were one of the few exotic foods that could withstand lengthy transport.

· Cloves trees grew only in a few Indonesian islands called the Spice Islands until very recently, providing a natural monopoly to spice traders.

· It is said that all of the clove trees in the rest of the world are descended from a still-living 400-year-old tree named Afo, whose seedlings were stolen in the 1700s.

# Coriander

Coriander is the seed of the cilantro plant, a member of the umbel family native to the Mediterranean. Despite coming from the same organism as the cilantro herb, coriander flavor is quite distinct and earthy.

## FORMS

· Coriander comes in seed pods and ground powder, but not loose seeds.

· The seeds are quite small and difficult to remove from the pods, so ground coriander is a mixture of seeds and pod fiber.

## COOKING

· Coriander powder is milder than most spices; don't be afraid to use somewhat large amounts.

· When frying or stir-frying, try adding whole coriander seeds to the oil as it is heating up, before adding any other ingredients. The coriander will flavor the oil.

## FRYING SEEDS

· Most of the flavorful compounds in coriander (and other seeds) are fat soluble. This means that flavors will stay trapped in the seed pod (and not be very tasty) unless they are first dissolved in oil.

· To get the most out of flavorful seeds, fry them in oil on a low heat for a few minutes before adding them to food. The seeds will flavor the oil, and the oil will flavor everything else.

· Not much oil is needed, since seeds are tiny. Use enough to just barely cover the seeds.

## SYNERGIES

· Coriander goes well in soups, stews, and stir-fries, especially in dishes with lots of protein.

· Coriander is a staple of curry mixes. Try spicing beans with coriander, cumin, turmeric, ginger, garlic, onions, and hot peppers.

· It can be nice to add a pinch of coriander to boiled grains.

· Try slowly simmering seeds with oil and an onion or two while you are boiling soup. Combine the two together right before serving for an unusually flavorful broth.

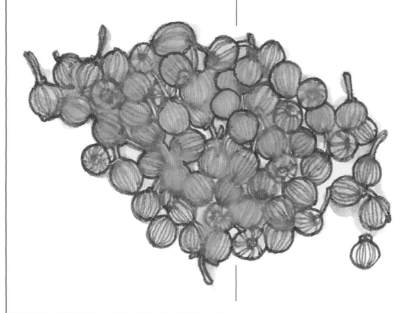

# Cumin

The cumin plant is a member of the umbel family native to the Middle East. Cumin spice is derived from the seeds and hard seed coat (the fruit) of the plant. Cumin is used heavily in Middle Eastern and Indian cooking and is largely responsible for the earthy undertones of most curries.

## FORMS

· Cumin can be found as whole seeds or as a ground powder.

· Whole seeds are preferable because they stay aromatic for longer. The seeds can be ground in a coffee grinder if powder is desired for a more uniform distribution of flavor, but if whole seeds are cooked for long enough, their flavor too will distribute fairly evenly.

## COOKING

· Cumin flavor is strong but not spicy. It's difficult to overwhelm a dish with cumin flavor, so don't be afraid of adding too much.

· When frying or stir-frying, try adding whole cumin seeds to the oil as it is heating up, before adding any other ingredients. The cumin will flavor the oil.

## SYNERGIES

· Cumin goes well in soups, stews, and stir-fries, especially in dishes with lots of protein.

· Cumin is a staple of curry mixes. Try spicing beans with cumin, coriander, turmeric, ginger, garlic, onions, and hot peppers.

· Powdered cumin can be nice to add to pasta. Try making a pasta sauce out of oil, cumin, and nutritional yeast.

· Try adding cumin to a tray of roasting vegetables like carrots, zucchini, or eggplant.

### UMBEL FLAVORS

· The seeds of many plants in the umbel family have rich and similar flavors. These seeds include cumin, coriander, fennel, caraway, dill, and celery.

· All of these seeds contain related fat-soluble compounds and have similar flavors.

· When spicing dishes, its often nice to mix many umbel seeds together. Their flavors will mix and complement each other quite nicely.

· Don't forget to fry the seeds in oil before adding them to your food, so the flavors can dissolve into the oil.

# Nutmeg

Nutmeg comes from the large seed of an evergreen tree native to a small archipelago in Indonesia. The seed is covered by a bright red webbing that is ground into the spice mace. The nutmeg fruit is also edible.

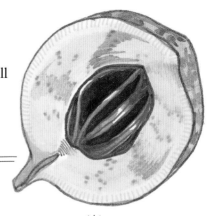

## FORMS

· Nutmeg is usually found in a powdered form since the whole seed is quite hard and difficult to grind by hand.

· Whole seeds have a stronger and fresher flavor than preground nutmeg. Seeds can be hand ground using a fine cheese grater.

## COOKING

· Nutmeg flavor is strong and quite distinctive. It synergizes with both sweet and savory foods, but its unique flavor makes it somewhat difficult to blend nicely with other flavorers. Use nutmeg sparingly and very deliberately.

· Nutmeg is most commonly used in sweet, creamy, fruity dishes.

## SYNERGIES

· Nutmeg works surprisingly well with eggs—it brings out highlights you wouldn't expect and works well with other egg flavorers.

· Stir a bit of nutmeg into applesauce or fruit compote.

· Try adding a pinch of nutmeg to fruit smoothies.

· Nutmeg can be a nice addition to dessert breads or muffins.

### NUTMEG HISTORY

· In the 1600s there was vicious competition between the European powers for control of the spice trade.

· Nutmeg trees grew only on a small chain of islands called the Bandas in Indonesia.

· In 1621, the Dutch East India Company mascaraed and enslaved the native population of the Bandas, which allowed them to maintain a monopoly on nutmeg production for the next century.

· Throughout most of its European history, nutmeg was a spice of conspicuous consumption, a table dressing that could only be afforded by the rich. Only in the past few hundred years has the price of nutmeg dropped as more trees were planted in other parts of the world.

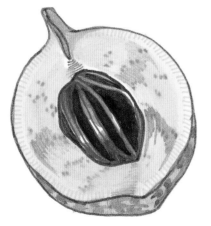

# Nutritional Yeast

Nutritional yeast is a yeast culture grown on sugar that has been baked so that the yeast is no longer biologically active, that is, no longer alive. Nutritional yeast is very high in protein and B vitamins, so it is often used by vegans as an ethical source of protein. It is also an excellent flavorer in its own right.

## FORMS

· Nutritional yeast is grown on large sheets and then broken up into flakes.

· Nutritional yeast texture ranges from small flakes to a fine powder, depending on its age and how much it's been moved around.

## COOKING

· Nutritional yeast has a thickening effect on food. Add it to soups, stews, and stir-fries to make them creamier, heavier, and heartier.

· Nutritional yeast can be used in small quantities with other spices to produce a particular flavor palate, or on its own in larger quantities as a condiment.

## SYNERGIES

· Nutritional yeast tastes quite cheesy and goes great on toast or pasta.

· One of the best uses for nutritional yeast is as a topping for popcorn. Nothing can quite match it.

· Add nutritional yeast to tomato sauce to make it heavier and more savory.

· Nutritional yeast is a great addition to lentil soup.

· Consider topping pizza with a mixture of cheese and nutritional yeast.

· Nutritional yeast is a great topping for most carbohydrates. Try sprinkling a bit on toast or pasta with butter.

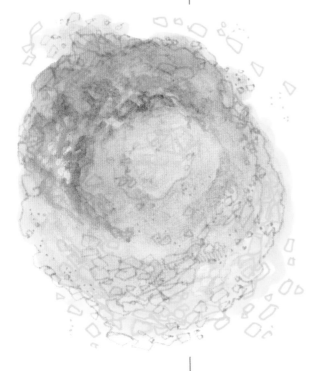

# Paprika

Paprika is a mixture of bell and hot peppers that have been dried and ground into a powder. Paprika has been made all over Europe since the introduction of the Mexican pepper there in the 1500s, most famously in Hungary.

## FORMS

· Because paprika is made by mixing different kinds of peppers together, the flavor varies greatly with the ratios of pepper used.

· Paprika ranges from sweet and mild to quite spicy but will always be a rich red powder.

## COOKING

· Paprika is useful when you want to add some spicy highlights to your dish, without making "hot" the dominant flavor. The milder forms of paprika will add zesty texture without overwhelming heat.

· Because paprika can be quite mild, it works great as a natural food coloring. The deep red is picked up easily by oils and grains. Paprika is almost better used as a food coloring than as a spice; good use of color and aesthetics can have a profound impact on the quality of a dish.

· Make sure to taste your paprika before adding it to food. Varieties differ in strength a great deal, and it's difficult to salvage a dish that is too hot.

· If you do end up adding too much paprika, try mixing in dairy or sweeteners. Dairy tends to even out the flavor and absorb some of the spiciness, while sweeteners add complexity and balance.

## SYNERGIES

· Try making a sauce from olive oil, paprika, and sour citrus that can be used on pasta or artichoke.

· The tiniest sprinkling of paprika on sliced fruit can add a little kick and variety in color.

· Paprika is a great addition to chicken broth.

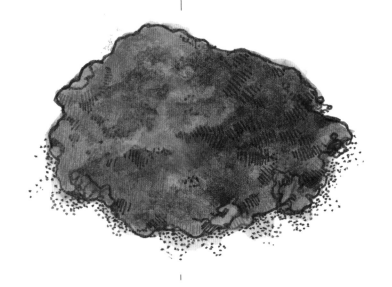

# Pepper

Pepper is the small seed and hard seed coat (the fruit) of a flowering vine native to India. Pepper has a long history as the centerpiece of the ancient global spice trade. When Spanish explorers (looking for alternate spice routes) brought hot peppers back to Europe, they called them peppers due to their similarity in taste to Old World pepper, even though the plants are completely different.

## FORMS

· Pepper comes in many colors, depending on how it is processed.

· Black peppercorns are pepper fruits that have been boiled and dried. White peppercorns are just the seed with the fruit removed. In other colored peppercorns, like green or red, the fruit has been pickled, fermented, or otherwise preserved.

· Pepper can be found as whole peppercorns or in ground form. Whole peppercorns stay flavorful for longer than ground pepper but are too large to cook with effectively and should be ground in a coffee grinder before use.

## COOKING

· Pepper is quite spicy but it doesn't add the same kind of heat that hot peppers do.

· When frying or stir-frying, try adding whole peppercorns to the oil as it is heating up, before adding any other ingredients. The pepper will flavor the oil. Be wary, though, that with this method it's likely that you'll end up biting into a whole peppercorn as you eat, which tends to be rather alarming.

· A bit of pepper goes well on most things, but be careful about adding too much.

## SYNERGIES

· Pepper is a suitable addition to most vegetable dishes.

· Pepper is a welcome flavor in most carbohydrates, especially boiled grains and pasta.

· Try adding a little pepper and ginger to baking tempeh for a spicy kick without much heat.

# Salt

Salt is an ionically bonded crystal made from sodium and chlorine. A small amount of salt is essential to keep the body functioning well, and so in ancient times when transportation was more difficult, salt was exceedingly valuable. The word *salary* actually derives from "salt," as Roman soldiers were often paid their salary in salt.

### FORMS

· Salt is most often extracted from seawater through evaporation or boiling, but the planet is also dotted with salt mines, full of salt deposits left from ancient seas that have been buried under mountains for millennia. These salt mines have been particularly important in remote places like Tibet, where the geography prevents people from accessing salt made from seawater.

· A minority of the salt produced in the world is actually consumed by humans. Most salt is used in chemical manufacturing processes and so is refined into pure sodium chloride. Since the 1920s, many governments have been adding iodine to this refined salt (iodized salt) to prevent iodine deficiencies.

· Many artisanal salts are available (from specific salt mines or ocean sources) that emphasize their natural mineral content—usually calcium, magnesium, and iron (which can give salt a pink hue!).

### COOKING

· It's easy to oversalt food. Try to add salt toward the end of cooking, once other spices have been added, to ensure that the salt isn't overpowering.

· The ideal amount of salt in a dish is often a matter of personal taste. When cooking for a large group, try to undersalt the food and let people add a bit more if they want.

· Salt is an essential ingredient in many preservative processes like pickling or smoking. Coating food with salt dehydrates it, making the surface difficult for bacteria to colonize. Humans have large, watery digestive tracts that can handle high quantities of salt. Bacteria don't, so they tend to stay away from very salty food. When pickling vegetables, don't skimp on the salt!

· Salt is water soluble, so it will evenly coat your food even if you use large crystals. Salt added to an individual serving doesn't get much of a chance to dissolve, however, so make sure your table salt is fine grained.

### SYNERGIES

· A small amount of salt is added to most food that isn't sweet.

· Sprinkle eggplant or zucchini slices with salt before cooking them. The salt dehydrates them and concentrates flavors.

· Sometimes it's nice to just sprinkle a little bit of salt on a salad instead of using a heavy dressing.

# Seeds

Most spices are derived from seeds. While some seeds have distinct flavors that are used for specific effect, many seeds have mild flavors and are used predominantly for texture. This page details seeds used for textural purposes.

## FORMS

**Sesame seeds**—pale, almond shaped, imperceptible flavor, used in tahini

**Poppy seeds**—small, round, black, mild nutty flavor

**Flax seeds**—deep brown, smooth, shiny, imperceptible flavor, slightly slimy when cooked

**Mustard seeds**—small, round, brown, slight mustard flavor

**Fennel seeds**—long, ribbed, gray-green, moderate licorice flavor

**Celery seeds**—small, oblong, ribbed, pale brown, mild coriander flavor

**Chia seeds**—shiny, speckled gray, imperceptible flavor, slimy when cooked

**Caraway seeds**—long, ribbed, gray, nutty flavor

## COOKING

· Some seeds are more flavorful than others. Chia, poppy, sesame, and flax can be difficult to taste and are used exclusively for added texture.

· Other seeds, like mustard, celery, and fennel (most of all), do have distinct flavors and can be used in large quantities as spices. In small amounts, they mostly add crunch.

· When frying or stir-frying, try adding fennel, mustard, or celery to the oil as it is heating up, before adding any other ingredients. The seeds will flavor the oil.

· Chia and flax seeds contribute not only crunch but lubrication. They both release a mucilaginous slime when mixed with water that coats food and helps it bind together. Because of this quality, and their high omega oil content, these seeds are often ground and whipped in water to create a vegan egg substitute.

· Seeds make a great addition to vegetable stir-fries. They add a decent amount of protein and break up the soft vegetable texture with their crunch.

· Seeds are aesthetically useful not just for texture but for color. Seeds (light or dark) break up homogeneous dishes by adding polka dots.

# Soy Sauce, Tamari

Soy sauce is a salty sauce made by fermenting a paste of wheat, soy, and salt in barrels for over a year and then extracting the liquid. The traditional process was developed in China about 2,000 years ago, and since then, the method has spread to most Asian countries, with distinct cultural adaptations.

### FORMS

· Soy sauce varieties differ in ratios of soy to wheat or other grains, the specific fermented species used, and the treatment process.

· Tamari is a Japanese variety that uses no wheat, so it is popular among people with gluten sensitivities. That said, even wheat-containing soy sauce varieties do not contain detectable quantities of gluten, as the protein is destroyed in the yearlong fermentation process.

· Some varieties, like the liquid aminos sold in health food stores or the type found in Chinese restaurant packets, are not fermented at all but rather are treated with acid to produce a similar breakdown of the soybean.

### COOKING

· Soy sauce contains a high quantity of amino acids. The amino content produces a meaty umami flavor. It imparts a heavier, more complex and savory flavor than salt alone.

· Because soy sauce is liquid, it coats food more easily than salt grains. It is often preferred as a table condiment over salt for this reason.

· Soy sauce is useful in stir-fries, where its distinct flavor is noticeable and its water content helps cook the food. In stews and soups, the subtle umami is usually dominated by other flavors, so salt works just as well.

### SYNERGIES

· The umami of soy sauce adds the illusion of savory weight to vegetable dishes.

· Soy sauce works well with boiled grains.

· Tempeh and tofu are particularly suited to soy sauce, as they are all soy products.

· Try spicing beans with onions, garlic, soy sauce, ginger, and pepper.

# Vanilla

Vanilla is derived from the seeds and pod of the vanilla orchid, a beautiful flowering plant native to Mexico. Vanilla production was isolated to Mexico, the only region where its bee pollinator lived, until the 1800s, when a hand pollination technique was developed by a slave in Madagascar.

## FORMS

· Vanilla "beans" are actually not beans but long black seed pods that are the fruit of the orchid.

· Vanilla is most commonly found in the form of vanilla extract. The seed pods are soaked in alcohol until the flavorful compounds in the pod, notably vanillin, have been absorbed, turning the liquid a deep brown.

· Vanilla extract is quite simple to make from whole vanilla beans—just soak them in hard alcohol for a few weeks.

· Vanillin is an easily manufactured by-product of the papermaking process, so artificial vanilla extract made from manufactured vanillin is quite cheap.

· Imitation vanilla extract is often mixed with castoreum to give it a complex flavor more similar to natural vanilla. Castoreum is a mixture of extremely potent aromatic compounds found within beaver anus scent glands, often listed on imitation vanilla ingredient labels as "natural flavors."

## COOKING

· Vanilla has a very smooth and subtle flavor that tends to stay in the background, underneath sharper tastes.

· That said, vanilla is a very strong spice and just a sprinkling is needed to make any dish taste distinctly of vanilla.

· Vanilla works best with sweet foods, mostly fruit and dairy, and spices that mix well with sweeteners.

## SYNERGIES

· Try mixing a little vanilla into plain yogurt. The vanilla is much more noticeable this way than in preflavored vanilla yogurts.

· Vanilla is a nice addition to oatmeal or coffee.

· Consider adding the lightest sprinkling of vanilla extract onto baking squash.

# Vinegar

The chemical name of vinegar is acetic acid. Vinegar is a waste product of a family of fermentive bacteria that get their energy by converting ethanol (alcohol) into acetic acid. Most vinegars are produced through an extension of the alcoholic fermentation process. One bacterial species ferments sugar into alcohol, and another ferments alcohol into vinegar.

## FORMS

· Vinegars can be differentiated by the sugar source they started from. Most vinegars contain a mixture of organic compounds that come from their original sugar source or bacterial fermenters that give the vinegar its distinct flavor.

· The exception is distilled white vinegar, which is pure acetic acid made by a complex industrial process. White vinegar usually starts as corn, but by the end of the process, nothing is left but water and about 5 percent acetic acid. Stronger solutions can be acquired but should not be used for culinary purposes.

· Balsamic vinegar is made by a lengthy artisanal manufacturing process where wine in barrels is converted into vinegar over the course of many years. All vinegar that is certified as "balsamic" was made in the Italian province of Modena.

· Apple cider vinegar is made by fermenting, you guessed it, hard apple cider.

· Rice vinegar is made from rice wine. Rice vinegar is nice because it tends to be lighter than balsamic or apple cider vinegar but still has a flavor more complex than white vinegar.

## COOKING

· Vinegar is used to make food taste sour. It can be used as a replacement for sour citrus, although flavor undertones can vary greatly.

· Vinegar has been used for millennia as a preservative. Its high acid content prevents most bacteria from growing. Most fruits and vegetables can be pickled by soaking them in vinegar, most popularly cucumbers and radishes. If stored properly, pickled food can last unrefrigerated for several years.

## SYNERGIES

· It is sometimes nice to add a dash of vinegar to stir-fries or salads, but make sure to use just a tiny amount. It's easy to overwhelm a dish with sourness.

· Vinegar is useful for cooking vegetables that are overly fibrous, like collard greens, cabbage, okra, or lotus root. Boiling very fibrous foods in a small amount of vinegar helps break down the fiber better than heat alone.

· Try mixing a dash of sweet vinegar, like rice or balsamic, into boiled grains.

# herbs

HERBS ARE SPICES that come exclusively from the leaves of plants. Unlike spices that come from seeds or other sources, herbs are best fresh. Avoid dried herbs since most of their taste is lost in the drying process. Fresh herbs can be kept refrigerated for about a week. The flavor of fresh herbs is subtle and easily overpowered. To really highlight an herb's taste in a dish, use much more plant matter than would be expected, especially when cooking with heat. Herbs are leaves, so it is very easy to overcook them and destroy most of their flavor. Add herbs to hot dishes at the very end of the cooking process to preserve their unique taste. Like other spices, effective use of herbs requires creativity and experimentation. Don't be afraid to add them in unexpected places. Herbs are incredibly useful for their aesthetic value—sticking a sprig of fresh herbs on the side of a serving bowl can add great appeal.

# Basil

Basil is an herb in the mint family native to Southeast Asia. Basil contains a diverse mixture of aromatic compounds, and its flavor can vary greatly. Cultivars contain varying proportions of chemicals also found in clove, citrus, and licorice.

## STORAGE

· Basil should be kept refrigerated and will keep for about a week.

· Freshly cut basil will keep in a glass of water for a few days.

· Basil can be dried, but dried basil loses most of its flavor.

## COOKING

· Basil should never be cooked for more than a minute or so, as heat destroys its flavor. Add basil at the very end of cooking, once the heat is turned off.

· **To make pesto**: Blend a mixture of basil, salt, garlic, and oil in a food processor until it becomes green and creamy. If you are low on basil, the pesto can be bulked with other herbs like sage or mint or even more mild leafy greens like spinach or lettuce. Nuts can be added for an earthy touch. Use pesto as pasta sauce or a bread spread.

· Wilting basil leaves and unwanted basil stems go great in soup stock.

## SYNERGIES

· Raw basil leaves go great in salad, especially with fresh tomatoes and cheese.

· Chopped basil makes a great garnish to pasta or boiled grains.

· Try cooking chicken in coconut milk and sour citrus and add some basil leaves at the end.

# Bay Leaves

Bay leaves are the dried aromatic leaves of a number of tropical evergreen trees. Bay leaves contain many aromatic essential oils, but the leaves themselves are quite hard, even after cooking, so they are not typically eaten.

## STORAGE

· Unlike other herbs, some kinds of bay leaves actually become more aromatic when they are dried.

· Bay leaves can be kept dried for several months, although flavor wanes with age.

## COOKING

· Bay leaves are almost always boiled into soups or stews and then removed before eating. The leaves are very fibrous and unpleasant to eat.

· It takes a long time for bay leaf flavors to leach into food. Only add bay leaves to food that will be boiling for more than half an hour.

· Bay leaf can be ground into a powder and sprinkled on food.

· Bay leaves make a great addition to soup stock.

## SYNERGIES

· A bay leaf or two is usually added to boiling beans.

· Try adding a bay leaf to tomato sauce.

· Bay leaves can be used in stuffing for baking poultry.

## ESSENTIAL OILS

· Bay leaves get their shinny look from a particularly large amount of essential oils.

· All herbs (and most other plants) have essential oils, but they're not in the bay leaf to make your soup taste good. Essential oils are a defense against predators. Animals that take a bite of bay leaf are put off by its extremely bitter taste and move on to munch on something else.

· Only humans have figured out that in very small quantities the essential oils in bay leaves can make food taste delicious.

# Cilantro

Cilantro is a soft herb in the umbel family native to the Mediterranean. Cilantro seeds are used as the spice coriander, although the two taste distinctly different. A small percentage of the population detests cilantro—to them it tastes like bitter soap. This is likely due to human genetic differences in taste and smell receptors. Most people find the taste of cilantro mild and fresh.

## STORAGE

· Cilantro should be kept refrigerated and will keep for a few days.

· Freshly cut cilantro will also keep in a glass of water for a few days.

· Cilantro can be dried, but dried cilantro loses most of its flavor.

## COOKING

· The flavor of cilantro is extremely delicate, and cilantro should never be cooked for more than a few seconds. Sprinkle chopped cilantro over your food once cooking is done.

· Because cilantro elicits a strong negative reaction from some people, if you are cooking for a group, it's a good idea to offer a bowl of cilantro as a side topping instead of mixing it into your food.

· Cilantro stems are edible and quite flavorful. They go great in salad.

## SYNERGIES

· Cilantro can add variety to the flavor of salads. Try making a dressing with cilantro and sour citrus.

· It's nice to chop up cilantro and parsley and use the leaves as a garnish for meat, especially fish.

· Cilantro's flavor is delicate enough that it can be a nice source of green in fruit salad.

# Dill

Dill is a thin-leafed herb in the umbel family native to eastern Europe. Dill is often relegated to specific dishes like fish or pickles, but in actuality, dill is a quite versatile herb and can add a surprising splash of flavor in unexpected places.

## STORAGE

· Dill should be kept refrigerated and will keep for about a week.

· Freshly cut dill will keep in a glass of water for a few days.

· Dill can be dried, but dried dill loses most of its flavor.

## COOKING

· Dill should never be cooked for more than a minute or so as heat destroys its flavor. Add dill at the very end of cooking, once the heat is turned off.

· Dill stems are edible and taste just like the leaves.

· Dill goes well with sour ingredients.

## SYNERGIES

· Raw dill goes great in salad, especially with a vinegar dressing.

· Try sprinkling a bit of dill on pasta with cheese.

· Dill can add a slightly cooling hint to spicy curries.

· Try making a bean dip with leftover beans and lots of dill.

· Fresh dill is a great addition to mashed potatoes or other root vegetables.

· Instead of fruit and sweeteners, try making a savory yogurt snack with dill and nuts.

# Lavender

Lavender is an herb in the mint family native to the Mediterranean. Lavender is particularly aromatic and is widely used as a perfume and decoration as well as an herb. The lavender flower is the source of the color word *lavender*.

## STORAGE

· Lavender should be kept refrigerated and will keep for over a week.

· Freshly cut lavender can be kept in a glass of water for several days.

· Lavender dries quite well and will remain aromatic for several weeks.

## COOKING

· Although lavender is quite aromatic, its flavor is very mild and very large quantities need to be cooked with to produce noticeable flavor.

· Lavender should never be cooked for more than a minute or so as heat destroys its flavor. Add lavender at the very end of cooking, once the heat is turned off.

· Lavender (dried or fresh) boils wonderfully into tea.

· Lavender contributes uniquely to both sweet and savory palates. It is often blended with dairy products and used in confections.

## SYNERGIES

· Try boiling rice with lavender. Its flavor will suffuse the grains.

· Oddly enough, lavender is well suited to yogurt. Chop it finely and mix it with yogurt, vanilla, and maybe maple syrup.

· Lavender is nice with delicate greens like chard or spinach, along with ginger, oil, and salt.

# Mint

Mint is a diverse genus of plants that grow on every continent of the world. The flavor of mint comes largely from the compound menthol, which unlike most flavors, actually binds to temperature receptors in your mouth, producing a cold sensation.

### STORAGE

· Mint should be kept refrigerated and will keep for about a week.

· Freshly picked mint can be kept in a glass of water for several days.

· Mint can be dried. Dried mint is most useful for making tea.

### COOKING

· Mint is best known for producing cold sensations, but different varieties can also taste sweet or sour.

· Mint is an excellent herb to use for tea. Dried mint confers its flavor to the water better, but the flavor of fresh mint is milder and more complex. When making tea with fresh mint, use a large quantity, about enough to fill the cup you are using. Chop the mint finely and boil it for a couple of minutes before drinking. Fresh mint can be steeped in hot water like regular tea, but the flavor will not be as strong.

### SYNERGIES

· Fresh mint leaves make an excellent addition to fruit salads or green salads. It goes well with sweet and sour food.

· Mint is often pulverized and blended into salad dressings. Try blending a mixture of mint, oil, water, apple cider vinegar, and salt in a blender.

· Mint can be an interesting addition to pesto. Consider a multiherb pesto made with basil, mint, dill, garlic, salt, and oil.

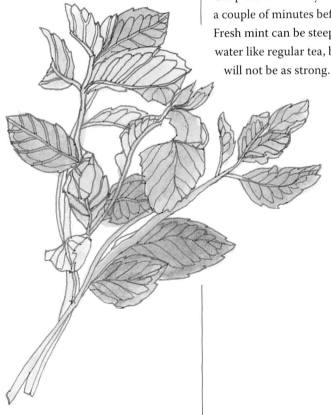

# Oregano

Oregano is a strong herb in the mint family native to the Mediterranean. Oregano is used heavily in Italian cooking and is responsible for the iconic flavor of pizza sauce.

## STORAGE

· Oregano can be kept refrigerated for about a week.

· Oregano is best when fresh, but dried oregano retains its flavor quite well and will keep for several weeks.

## COOKING

· Oregano should never be cooked for more than a couple of minutes, as heat destroys its flavor. Still, oregano withstands heat better than other herbs and ought to be cooked slightly before eating.

· Oregano can be quite strong and goes best with hearty foods. It does well with beans and meat.

· Oregano is perhaps the strongest of all common herbs. A little bit goes a long way.

· Wilting leaves and unwanted oregano stems go great in soup stock.

## SYNERGIES

· Oregano is a fantastic addition to tomato sauce.

· Try stuffing a chicken with oregano, rosemary, apples, and garlic.

· Oregano is nice to add to heavy bean chilies and curries.

# Parsley

Parsley is a frilly herb in the umbel family native to the Mediterranean. Some cultivars of parsley are grown for their thick taproot, which is similar to parsnip and carrot, also in the umbel family.

### STORAGE

· Parsley should be kept refrigerated and will keep for about a week.

· Freshly cut parsley will keep in a glass of water for a few days.

· Parsley can be dried, but dried parsley loses most of its flavor.

### COOKING

· Parsley is frequently used aesthetically as a garnish. Its flavor is quite mild—it mostly tastes fresh and green.

· Parsley should never be cooked for more than a minute or so, as heat destroys its flavor. Add parsley at the very end of cooking, once the heat is turned off.

· Wilting leaves and unwanted parsley stems go great in soup stock.

### SYNERGIES

· Raw parsley goes great in salad.

· If parsley is present in large enough quantities, it can be cooked as a leafy green along with kale and chard.

· Blend a mixture of garlic, oil, salt, and parsley together in a food processor to make a spicy bread spread called aioli.

# Rosemary

Rosemary is a woody evergreen herb in the mint family native to the Mediterranean. The name rosemary derives from the Latin words *ros* ("dew") and *marius* ("sea"). Rosemary is the dew of the sea, perhaps because of its drought resistance. Rosemary is very hearty, and its leaves are quite tough and waxy.

## STORAGE

· Rosemary should be refrigerated and will keep for several weeks.

· Rosemary dries much better than other herbs. Dried rosemary is quite flavorful and will keep for several months.

## COOKING

· Raw rosemary is actually slightly bitter. Rosemary needs to be cooked for its flavor to leach into food.

· Rosemary leaves are great baked with meat or root vegetables or boiled into soup or grains.

· Rosemary contains many flavorful essential oils that dissolve in and flavor fat. Try adding a few fresh leaves to the oil of a stir-fry as it is heating up.

· As fresh rosemary ages, its leaves tend to blacken. Black leaves should not be cooked with but can be used along with stems for soup stock.

## SYNERGIES

· Rosemary is suited to roasting, as it retains its flavor even when dry. Try baking rosemary on a bed of potatoes with lots of salt and oil.

· Rosemary makes a fine addition to scrambled eggs, along with spinach, onions, or mushrooms.

· To infuse cooking oil with rosemary, place a few sprigs inside a full oil bottle and let it sit for a few weeks. The rosemary will imbue the oil in its flavor. To speed up the process, heat the oil and rosemary sprigs on the stove for a few minutes. This speeds up the transfer of aromatic oils from the rosemary leaves to the cooking oil, but you run the risk of cooking away some of the more delicate flavors.

# Sage

Common sage, or green sage, is an herb in the mint family native to the Mediterranean. There are hundreds of different kinds of aromatic sages from all over the globe. Many, like *Salvia apiana* (white sage) and *Salvia divinorum* (salvia), are used for religious purposes.

## STORAGE

· Sage should be refrigerated and will keep for over a week.

· Sage can be dried, but dried sage loses much of its flavor.

## COOKING

· Sage has a delicate earthy flavor and requires some cooking before consumption, as the leaves are rather tough. Add it just at the end of cooking for a minute or two and stop heating the dish when the leaves soften and turn a deep, vibrant green. Don't let the sage leaves become too brown.

· Browning, wilting leaves and unwanted sage stems go great in soup stock.

· Sage can be boiled in water to make a mild tea.

## SYNERGIES

· Try making an omelet with sage, mushrooms, and butter.

· You can make a fatty sauce with sage, oil, garlic, and nutritional yeast that can be mixed into boiled grains like quinoa or amaranth.

· Sage is great to add to mung bean curry or lentil soup.

· Sage imparts its flavor to oil quite well. Try boiling sage in butter or oil for a few minutes to be used as a pasta sauce or stir-fry flavoring.

# Thyme

Thyme is a small, stemmy herb in the mint family native to the Mediterranean. The word *thyme* comes from an ancient Greek word meaning "burn as sacrifice." Thyme is highly aromatic and was often used in ancient times as a burning incense or perfume.

## STORAGE

· Thyme should be refrigerated and will keep for over a week.

· Thyme can be dried, but dried thyme loses most of its flavor.

## COOKING

· Thyme is fragrant and slightly astringent. It goes best in savory dishes with lots of protein.

· Thyme has very thin, woody stems, and it can be quite tedious to remove the leaves from the stalks. The easiest way is to hold the top of the stem and pull down tightly with a finger and thumb, but this is time consuming. Thyme can be cooked with the stems attached, but it must be removed from the dish before serving.

· Because thyme is rather difficult to process, the sprigs are often boiled in soup stock. This method imparts thyme flavor to the broth without the effort of separating the stems from the leaves.

· Thyme leaves can withstand more cooking than some herbs but should still be added toward the end of the cooking process, a few minutes before the heat is turned off.

## SYNERGIES

· Thyme is well suited to be cooked into tomato sauce, along with oregano and rosemary.

· Try adding thyme to meat dishes with maybe the tiniest hint of mint and horseradish.

· Thyme is an excellent addition to boiled beans.

# nutrition glossary

This is a glossary of commonly used nutritional buzzwords and what they mean.

**calorie:** This is a unit of energy. One calorie is the amount of energy it takes to raise the temperature of one kilogram of water one degree Celsius.

**carbohydrates:** These are organic compounds made from carbon, hydrogen, and oxygen (hence the name). Carbohydrates take many forms, roughly categorized as sugar, starch, and fiber.

**enzyme:** This is a chemical catalyst made out of protein. Enzymes produce an environment in which chemical reactions can take place in your body, but they are not consumed by the reaction. Thus, they are said to be catalysts—substances that take part in a chemical reaction but are not themselves reactants.

**fats:** These are organic compounds made from carbon and hydrogen, also called hydrocarbons. The oil that we eat, like olive oil, and the oil that we use for fuel, like gasoline, are both called oil for a reason. They are both hydrocarbons but with different internal structures. Fats are the most energy-dense food we eat, but they are also the most difficult to digest.

**fiber:** This is an organic compound made from many rings of sugar bonded together to form a chain. Fibers are different from starches because animals do not produce enzymes capable of digesting them—so humans can digest starch but not fiber. The most common fiber is cellulose, the material that plants make their bodies out of. Interestingly, some bacteria can and do digest cellulose. Those bacteria live in the guts of grazing animals and termites, among other creatures, allowing them to use energy from plant material that they could not otherwise acquire. Although humans cannot digest fiber, it is still a necessary nutrient. Fiber makes up a large portion of our waste, and we need its bulk to give our waste enough substance to pass through our large intestine.

**inorganic compound:** This is a molecule or ion that does not contain carbon.

**macronutrient:** This is a substance that provides energy when digested. The three kinds of macronutrients are carbohydrates, proteins, and fats.

**micronutrient:** This is a substance that provides a specific chemical needed for body maintenance and function. Micronutrients are roughly categorized as vitamins and minerals.

**mineral:** This is an inorganic compound or element with a specific biological function. Sodium, calcium, phosphorus, iron, potassium, and iodine are all common minerals.

**organic compound:** This is a molecule (compound) made from a chain of carbon atoms, with oxygen and hydrogen usually present in significant proportions. Other elements, like nitrogen, phosphorus, potassium, calcium, sulfur, sodium, and so on, are sometimes present in smaller proportions.

**proteins:** These are organic compounds made from amino acid chains. Proteins are more energy dense and chemically complex than carbohydrates. We need protein to produce enzymes and muscle tissue.

**starch:** This is an organic compound made from many rings of sugar bonded together to form a chain.

**sugar:** This is an organic compound made from carbon, hydrogen, and oxygen atoms bonded together to form a ring.

**vitamins:** A vitamin is a complex organic compound with a specific biological function, sometimes enzymatic. We only need small quantities of specific vitamins, but vitamin deficiencies can be fatal.

# cooking style glossary

**baking:** This is a cooking method that uses the dry heat of an oven to cook food, rather than heat through a fluid medium like steaming, boiling, frying, or stir-frying. Because baked food is not cooked in a fluid, it is important to make sure that the food itself contains enough moisture so that it doesn't dry out during the baking process. Baking food in a covered pan or wrapped in tinfoil is a common solution to this drying problem, but even then water or oil must be added in the beginning. The biggest difference between baking and stovetop cooking is that with baking, cooler, diffuse heat is applied to all sides, while on the stovetop, hotter direct heat is applied to the bottom only. Baking is a great method for large ingredients with low surface-area-to-volume ratios, like potatoes, bread, squash, and meat. The geometry of these types of foods prevents their insides from drying out. Baking allows the gentle heat of the oven to permeate the entire food and cook it to the core. This would not be possible on a stovetop, where ingredients need to be cut up in order to cook thoroughly. Baking is a slow process. It takes a long time for cooking temperature heat to reach the core of large baked ingredients.

**boiling:** This is perhaps the simplest cooking style. To boil food, simply cover it with water in a pot and heat it on the stove. With some foods that are very sensitive to moisture, like pasta, the water should be brought to a boil before the ingredient is added. Most of the time, however, ingredients can be added to cold water and slowly brought to a boil. When making soup with multiple ingredients, it is important to pay attention to cook time. Many vegetables are delicate and should only be boiled into soup for a few minutes, while protein and grains tend to require longer cook times.

**fermenting:** This is an ancient process by which we preserve food by transforming one ingredient into another one that breaks down less easily and is less subject to dangers from pests. Fermenting preserves our food because the beneficial bacteria we introduce outcompete the other organisms that cause rot. Fermentation allows us to take control of the inevitable process of decay—we choose the time frame and form into which our food breaks down. Fermentation unites us with life's most basic forms. Rather than curse the bacteria as agents of disease, we choose to ally ourselves with them. A symbiosis emerges—a mutually beneficial relationship in which both life forms prosper. The bacteria are provided with food and a place to live, and in return they transform our water into wine. With fermentation, even decay itself can be a cooking method.

**frying:** Frying food is like boiling it in oil. The hot oil soaks into the food and brings out unique flavors. To fry food, first fill a frying pan with enough oil to submerge what you are cooking. A half inch to inch of oil (1 to 3 cm) will usually suffice. Only use high-temperature oils, as lower-temperature oils will smoke and burn. Heat the oil for several minutes before adding any food. If you add food before the oil is hot, it will absorb too much oil before it is thoroughly cooked and taste overly heavy and greasy. Once the oil is hot, add your ingredients and let them sizzle for a few minutes. It is likely that the pan you are using has hotter regions and colder regions, especially if it is a large pan. Try to figure out which areas are the hottest and note that cook time will vary accordingly. Check the bottom of your food often and monitor color change. When the food turns golden brown, it's time to flip it.

When both sides are golden brown, quickly remove the food from the pan and place it on a plate covered in paper towels to absorb the extra oil. When done frying, the remaining oil can be saved in a jar and used to fry with again later.

**grilling:** Grilling is cooking food on a metal grate over an open flame. Commercial propane grills are popular, but I prefer to grill my food over an open campfire. Grilling imbues food with a distinctive smoky flavor. It is similar to stir-frying because the food is heated exclusively from below, but like baking, the heat is dry. There is no fluid in between the food and the flame, so it is easy to burn grilled food.

**juicing:** Juicing is a process in which water—and other water soluble parts of the food like sugars, vitamins, and minerals—is removed from the fibrous parts of the food that are bulky and difficult to digest. Most fruit can be juiced, especially water-heavy fruits like citrus and melons. Vegetables like carrots or spinach also make flavorful juice, but the juice volume will be fairly minimal compared to the original volume of the food. It is usually too expensive to buy food explicitly for juicing. Juicing should be considered predominantly a food preservation technique—a process saved for times when food is present in excess and can be used somewhat inefficiently. Fruit that is going bad can usually be salvaged by juicing it—the juice of over-soft, mealy fruits is often sweeter than ripe fruit juice. Fresh-squeezed juice is best when drunk right away, but it can also be frozen for later or fermented into homemade wine or apple cider. Both electronic and manual juicers usually produce very concentrated juice, so it's often a good idea to water it down a bit before drinking.

**roasting:** There is no fundamental difference between baking and roasting; the words are used interchangeably. By some definitions, roasted food is cooked in the oven without a cover, while baked food is covered, but this distinction is difficult to apply consistently. For the most part, the words are synonymous.

**steaming:** Steaming is very similar to boiling, except that the boiling water and the food are kept in separate compartments. A metal sieve of some kind separates the food from the boiling water. Steam from the water rises through the sieve, and the heat of the steam cooks the food. Steaming can also be accomplished without a sieve by boiling the ingredients with a very small amount of water, less than a half inch (1 cm). Most of the ingredient will not be submerged in such a small amount of water, and as the water boils, the unsubmerged portions will be steamed. With this method, it is important to stir the food constantly to prevent it from burning and sticking to the bottom of the pot.

**stir-frying:** Stir-frying is like a combination of steaming and frying. Stir-fries use a combination of oil and water to cook food. Both liquids act as a medium to transfer heat from the burner to the food, but each works slightly differently. The water boils into steam that cooks food very evenly, but it tends to leave ingredients tasteless and soggy. Oil, on the other hand, makes food crispy and brings out more flavor than water alone. However, oil can burn food easily and can also make it overly heavy and fatty. Stir-frying allows you to use smaller, more healthy quantities of oil while still getting the taste benefits of frying. Stir-fries must be stirred constantly to ensure even cooking. In addition, the order in which ingredients are added is crucial. Stay aware of the various cook times each ingredient has, and add them in order of longest to shortest cook time so that nothing gets over- or undercooked. Stir-frying is my preferred method for cooking most things because it is very quick, and the taste produced is more balanced than either steaming or frying alone can provide.

# cooking style index

This index organizes ingredients by cooking method and arranges them in order of cook time. Cook times listed are vague estimations and will vary significantly based on age, ripeness, size, cultivar, and so on. However, the relative position of ingredients on the chart is quite accurate. That is, ingredients on the top of each list definitely take longer than those on the bottom.

| | STEAMING | |
|---|---|---|
| PAGE # | INGREDIENT NAME | APPROXIMATE COOK TIME |
| 40 | Pumpkin | 40 min |
| 16 | Artichoke | 30–45 min *varies with size* |
| 60 | Yam | 30 min |
| 60 | Taro | 30 min |
| 60 | Cassava | 30 min |
| 40 | Acorn squash | 25 min |
| 40 | Butternut squash | 25 min |
| 40 | Spaghetti squash | 25 min |
| 56 | Potato | 20 min |
| 61 | Sweet potato | 20 min |
| 18 | Beets | 20 min |
| 37 | Parsnip | 20 min |
| 37 | Turnip | 20 min |
| 21 | Brussels sprouts | 15 min |
| 22 | Cabbage | 10–30 min *varies with cultivar* |
| 32 | Kohlrabi | 13 min |
| 55 | Plantain | 12 min |
| 28 | Eggplant | 11 min |
| 39 | Zucchini | 10 min |
| 68 | Edamame | 10 min |
| 73 | Tempeh | 10 min |
| 29 | Fennel | 10 min |
| 23 | Carrot | 5–20 min *raw vs. mushy* |
| 27 | Collard greens | 7 min |
| 20 | Broccoli | 7 min |
| 24 | Cauliflower | 7 min |
| 30 | Green beans | 5–10 min *old beans take longer* |
| 35 | Okra | 6 min |
| 17 | Asparagus | 5 min |
| 31 | Kale | 5 min |
| 50 | Corn on the cob | 4 min |
| 26 | Chard | 4 min |
| 74 | Tofu | 4 min |
| 19 | Bell peppers | 3 min |
| 38 | Spinach | 1 min |

## STIR-FRYING

| PAGE # | INGREDIENT | APPROXIMATE COOK TIME |
|---|---|---|
| 71 | Beef | 20 min |
| 71 | Pork | 20 min |
| 71 | Lamb | 20 min |
| 71 | Goat | 20 min |
| 65 | Duck | 20 min |
| 65 | Turkey | 20 min |
| 65 | Chicken | 20 min |
| 70 | Swordfish | 20 min |
| 70 | Tuna | 20 min |
| 70 | Salmon | 20 min |
| 37 | Turnip | 20 min |
| 37 | Parsnip | 20 min |
| 18 | Beets | 20 min |
| 56 | Potato | 20 min *starch will get everywhere* |
| 22 | Cabbage | 10–20 min *depending on cultivar* |
| 23 | Carrots | 5–20 min *raw vs. mushy* |
| 28 | Eggplant | 15 min |
| 29 | Fennel | 15 min |
| 34 | Mushrooms | 10–15 min *can cook for longer* |
| 64 | Bacon | 10 min |
| 32 | Kohlrabi | 10 min |
| 73 | Tempeh | 10 min |
| 39 | Zucchini | 5–15 min *soft or crunchy* |
| 36 | Radish | 10 min |
| 21 | Brussels sprouts | 8 min |
| 20 | Broccoli | 7 min |
| 24 | Cauliflower | 7 min |
| 27 | Collard greens | 7 min |
| 30 | Green beans | 5–10 min *old beans take longer* |
| 17 | Asparagus | 6 min |
| 69 | Eggs | 5 min |
| 78 | Apples | 5 min |

## STIR-FRYING *continued*

| PAGE # | INGREDIENT | APPROXIMATE COOK TIME |
|---|---|---|
| 93 | Pineapple | 5 min |
| 31 | Kale | 5 min |
| 74 | Tofu | 5 min |
| 26 | Chard | 4 min |
| 19 | Bell peppers | 3 min |
| 38 | Spinach | 2 min |
| 72 | Nuts | 0–20 min *no need to cook* |
| 91 | Olives | 0–20 min *no need to cook* |
| 95 | Tomatoes | 0–10 min *raw vs. saucy* |

## FRYING

| PAGE # | INGREDIENT | APPROXIMATE COOK TIME |
|---|---|---|
| 60 | Taro | 20 min |
| 60 | Yam | 20 min |
| 60 | Cassava | 20 min |
| 71 | Beef | 20 min |
| 71 | Pork | 20 min |
| 71 | Lamb | 20 min |
| 71 | Goat | 20 min |
| 65 | Duck | 20 min |
| 65 | Turkey | 20 min |
| 65 | Chicken | 20 min |
| 74 | Tofu | 20 min |
| 56 | Potato | 15 min |
| 61 | Sweet potato | 10 min |
| 55 | Plantain | 10 min |
| 28 | Eggplant | 10 min |
| 64 | Bacon | 10 min |
| 73 | Tempeh | 10 min |
| 69 | Eggs | 5 min |
| 50 | Popcorn | 5 min |

## GRILLING

| PAGE # | INGREDIENT | APPROXIMATE COOK TIME |
|---|---|---|
| 71 | Beef | 30 min |
| 71 | Pork | 30 min |
| 71 | Lamb | 30 min |
| 71 | Goat | 30 min |
| 65 | Duck | 30 min |
| 65 | Turkey | 30 min |
| 65 | Chicken | 30 min |
| 70 | Swordfish | 20 min |
| 70 | Tuna | 20 min |
| 70 | Salmon | 20 min |
| 50 | Corn on the cob | 20 min |
| 28 | Eggplant | 20 min |
| 34 | Mushrooms | 15 min |
| 39 | Zucchini | 15 min |
| 17 | Asparagus | 10 min |
| 93 | Pineapple | 10 min |
| 73 | Tempeh | 10 min |
| 19 | Bell peppers | 5 min |

## BAKING

*Baking cook times vary extremely with size and oven temperature!*

| PAGE # | INGREDIENT | APPROXIMATE COOK TIME |
|---|---|---|
| 65 | Whole turkey | 180 min |
| 54 | Granola | 120 min *on very low heat* |
| 40 | Pumpkin | 120 min |
| 65 | Whole chicken | 120 min |
| 60 | Yam | 70 min |
| 60 | Taro | 70 min |
| 60 | Cassava | 70 min |
| 71 | Beef | 60 min |
| 71 | Pork | 60 min |
| 71 | Lamb | 60 min |

## BAKING *continued*

| PAGE # | INGREDIENT | APPROXIMATE COOK TIME |
|---|---|---|
| 71 | Goat | 60 min |
| 37 | Celery root | 60 min |
| 40 | Butternut squash | 60 min |
| 40 | Acorn squash | 60 min |
| 40 | Spaghetti squash | 60 min |
| 56 | Potato | 60 min |
| 61 | Sweet potato | 50 min |
| 37 | Parsnip | 45 min |
| 37 | Turnip | 45 min |
| 18 | Beets | 45 min |
| 69 | Egg quiche | 45 min |
| 22 | Cabbage | 40 min |
| 21 | Brussels sprouts | 40 min |
| 55 | Plantain | 30 min |
| 28 | Eggplant | 30 min |
| 39 | Zucchini | 30 min |
| 32 | Kohlrabi | 30 min |
| 29 | Fennel | 30 min |
| 23 | Carrot | 30 min |
| 74 | Tofu | 30 min |
| 73 | Tempeh | 30 min |
| 70 | Swordfish | 25 min |
| 70 | Tuna | 25 min |
| 70 | Salmon | 25 min |
| 64 | Bacon | 25 min |
| 19 | Bell peppers | 15–45 min *raw vs. soft inside/crunchy outside* |
| 95 | Tomatoes | 10–45 min *raw vs. soft inside/crunchy outside* |
| 17 | Asparagus | 20 min |
| 92 | Pears | 10 min |
| 93 | Pineapple | 10 min |
| 78 | Apples | 10 min |
| 72 | Nuts | 0–60 min *no need to cook* |

## BOILING

*Ingredients that need to be boiled for more than 45 minutes are difficult to overcook and can be boiled indefinitely.*

*Ingredients that need more than 15 minutes to cook fully can be cooked further if necessary, for almost an hour without much ill effect.*

| PAGE # | INGREDIENT | APPROXIMATE COOK TIME |
|---|---|---|
| 68 | Soybeans | 120 min |
| 65 | Whole turkey | 120 min |
| 66 | Black beans | 60–90 min |
| 66 | Red beans | 60–90 min |
| 66 | White beans | 60–90 min |
| 66 | Garbanzo beans | 60–90 min |
| 66 | Kidney beans | 60–90 min |
| 66 | Split peas | 60–90 min |
| 65 | Whole chicken | 60–90 min |
| 40 | Pumpkin | 60 min |
| 71 | Beef | 60 min |
| 71 | Pork | 60 min |
| 71 | Lamb | 60 min |
| 65 | Duck | 60 min |
| 67 | Adzuki beans | 45 min |
| 67 | Mung beans | 40 min |
| 37 | Celery root | 40 min |
| 60 | Yam | 40 min |
| 60 | Taro | 40 min |
| 60 | Cassava | 40 min |
| 40 | Butternut squash | 35 min |
| 40 | Acorn squash | 35 min |
| 45 | Barley | 35 min |
| 59 | Rice | 30–60 min *white vs. brown* |
| 16 | Artichoke | 30–40 min *depending on size* |
| 66 | Lentils | 35 min |
| 56 | Potato | 25 min |
| 37 | Parsnip | 25 min |
| 37 | Turnip | 25 min |
| 34 | Mushrooms | 25 min |
| 18 | Beets | 20 min *more is okay* |

## BOILING *continued*

| PAGE # | INGREDIENT | APPROXIMATE COOK TIME |
|---|---|---|
| 58 | Quinoa | 20 min |
| 61 | Sweet potato | 20 min |
| 70 | Tuna | 20 min |
| 70 | Salmon | 20 min |
| 70 | Swordfish | 20 min |
| 22 | Cabbage | 20 min |
| 28 | Eggplant | 20 min |
| 23 | Carrot | 10–30 min *raw vs. soft* |
| 52 | Millet | 20 min |
| 44 | Amaranth | 20 min |
| 21 | Brussels sprouts | 15 min |
| 32 | Kohlrabi | 15 min |
| 29 | Fennel | 15 min |
| 48 | Buckwheat | 10 min |
| 49 | Bulgur wheat | 10 min |
| 54 | Oatmeal | 10 min |
| 55 | Plantain | 10 min |
| 69 | Eggs | 10 min |
| 39 | Zucchini | 10 min |
| 36 | Radish | 9 min |
| 68 | Edamame | 9 min |
| 53 | Noodles | 5–20 min *easy to overcook* |
| 73 | Tempeh | 9 min |
| 24 | Cauliflower | 7 min |
| 20 | Broccoli | 7 min |
| 27 | Collard greens | 7 min |
| 17 | Asparagus | 6 min |
| 30 | Green beans | 5–10 min *old beans take longer* |
| 35 | Okra | 5 min |
| 31 | Kale | 5 min |
| 86 | Dried fruits | 5–10 min *soft vs. hard* |
| 26 | Chard | 4 min |
| 50 | Corn on the cob | 3 min |
| 74 | Tofu | 3 min |
| 95 | Tomatoes | 1–30 min *raw vs. sauce* |
| 38 | Spinach | 1 min |

# alphabetical index

# acknowledgments

## MAXIMUS THALER

I've read dozens of book acknowledgments, but I don't think I ever understood their importance until I sat down to write one. Writing is intensely collaborative. While I may be the sole author of this paragraph of gratitude, I am in no way the sole author of this book. *A Curious Harvest* was decidedly a group effort, and all of the collaborators deserve mutual appreciation. Many thanks to my editor Jonathan; if you had not invited yourself over to Crafty dinner for reasons I'm still not completely clear on, this book would not have happened. My appreciation for Dayna is difficult to put into words. You were there before the beginning and will be here after the end. You drew beets with me after midnight wearing an imaginary business suit. Having you by my side, even when neither of us knew where we were going, has made me feel immeasurably lucky. Paul is in some ways the inspiration for all of this. Thank you for teaching me the fine art of finding wealth in the trash. And thanks to Felipe for showing me on a cold week in January just how easy it is to eat exclusively from a Dumpster. Thanks to my mother for instilling in me a strong sense of nutrition and to my father for showing me how to build a house out of scraps. Thanks to Jeff and Fede and Bread and Puppet for teaching me how to make food last while making sure that everyone has enough to eat and for giving me the opportunity to cook good food for good people, every day, and learn while doing it. Penultimately, I want to thank all the people who helped me with The Gleaners' Kitchen: Rebecca, Kunle, Patrick, and especially Nick and Rachael. Nick, your dedication and commitment is astounding. You put in so many long hours and worked hardest when things were bleakest. I can't thank you enough. Rachael, without you I don't think there would have been a Gleaners' Kitchen at all. You provided support and inspiration, kindness, care, and love. You were my home when I felt the most homeless. Thank you.

Lastly and perhaps most importantly, I have to thank the Crafts House. Not the people, the Crafties, although my friendship with many of you will last lifetimes, but the house itself. The aesthetics and ethics of Crafts House had a more profound effect on me than any other single entity in my life. You are in many ways like my mother; I spent four years inside of you, growing from your nourishment, and I will take part of you with me wherever I go. You were a prototype for the home and community that I will spend the rest of my life seeking. I hope that a copy of this book can remain in the Crafty kitchen for many, many years to come.

## DAYNA SAFFERSTEIN

Thank you to everyone who helped me turn my passionate loves for eating and drawing into my very first book. Of course, to Maximus: you made my dreams come true. To Jonathan for coming to dinner and seeing a gem in our Dumpstered concoctions. To everyone who let me balance a pineapple on their living room table or who didn't blink an eye when I pulled out a cassava root on the subway and started sketching. To Leslie Salisbury for lending me your tempeh and the Hartungs for taking me to the beach, where I drew most of the cheeses, and then eating the sandy cheeses with me after. To those who helped me get through the dark age: you know who you are. To Allison and Arcadia for buying me the big girl bowl. But most of all this book is for Crafts House. Crafts House, you are my haven, my magic place. Crafties, you are my soul mates. May our time shared between painted walls and mountains of dishes live on forever through this book.

# about the authors

**MAXIMUS THALER** graduated from Tufts University in 2013, where he studied alchemy, biology, art, physics, and philosophy, with a minor in communal living and Dumpster diving. His cooking style and food ethics are influenced by the Bread and Puppet Theatre and also a general appreciation for what grows in the dirt. More information on Dumpstering can be found at thegleanerskitchen.org.

**DAYNA SAFFERSTEIN** lives in Brooklyn, New York, for the moment. She graduated in 2013 from the School of the Museum of Fine Arts, Boston, and Tufts University, where she specialized in illustration and screenprinting. Her favorite things to draw are vegetables, car fresheners, and yetis. She has a voracious appetite. Visit her online at daynasafferstein.com.

# also available

**THE KITCHEN PANTRY COOKBOOK**
978-1-59253-843-0

**GOING RAW**
978-1-59253-685-6

**REAL FOOD FERMENTATION**
978-1-59253-784-6

**HOMEGROWN SPROUTS**
978-1-59253-870-6

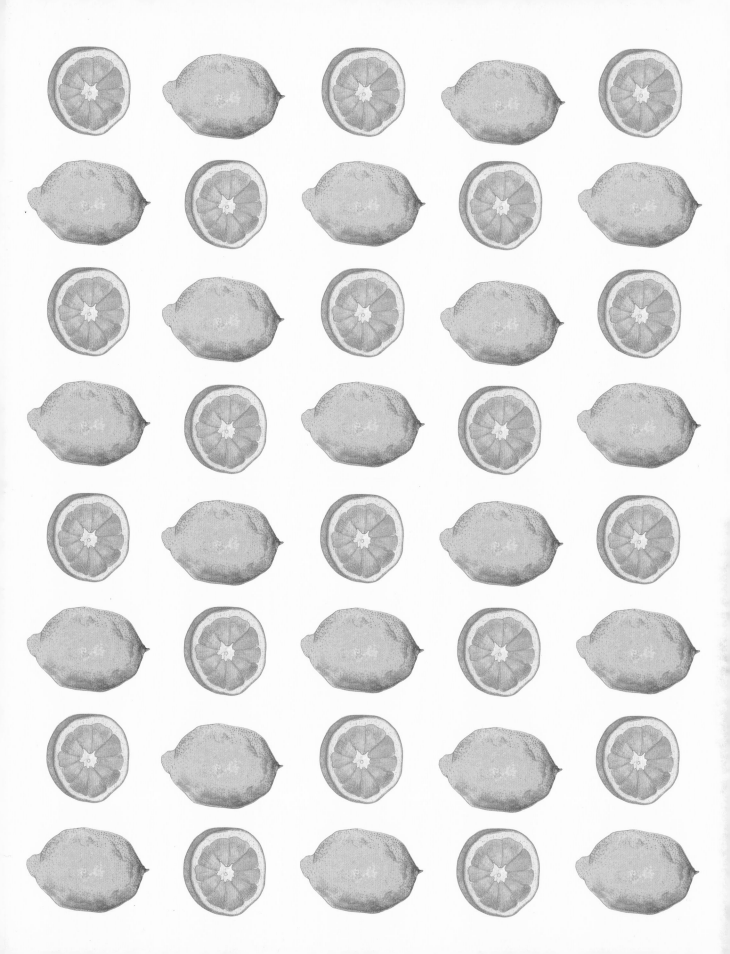